Office of Government Commerce

Passing your ITIL® Foundation Exam

London: TSO

information & publishing solutions

Published by TSO (The Stationery Office) and available from:

Online
www.tsoshop.co.uk

Mail, Telephone, Fax & E-mail
TSO
PO Box 29, Norwich, NR3 1GN
Telephone orders/General enquiries: 0870 600 5522
Fax orders: 0870 600 5533
E-mail: customer.services@tso.co.uk
Textphone 0870 240 3701

TSO Shops
16 Arthur Street, Belfast BT1 4GD
028 9023 8451 Fax 028 9023 5401
71 Lothian Road, Edinburgh EH3 9AZ
0870 606 5566 Fax 0870 606 5588

TSO@Blackwell and other Accredited Agents

Published for the Office of Government Commerce under licence from the Controller of Her Majesty's Stationery Office.

First published 2007

Second impression, with corrections 2008

ISBN 9780113310791

Printed in the United Kingdom by The Stationery Office
N5739997 c60 04/08

Contents

List of figures   v

List of tables   vii

OGC's foreword   viii

Chief Examiner's foreword   ix

The Official Accreditor's foreword   x

Acknowledgements   xi

1 The ITIL Qualification Scheme: professional qualifications for ITIL practices for Service Management   1

1.1 Three levels of qualification   3

1.2 Qualifications bodies   5

1.3 The ITIL Foundation certificate in IT Service Management   6

1.4 About this publication   7

2 Service Management as a practice   9

2.1 Services   11

2.2 Service Management   12

2.3 Resources and capabilities   13

2.4 Utility and warranty   13

2.5 Service Packages   14

2.6 Processes, functions and roles   15

2.7 Good practice   21

2.8 Sample questions and answers   21

3 The Service Lifecycle   23

3.1 The ITIL Service Management Practices   25

3.2 The Service Lifecycle   25

3.3 Sample question and answer   26

4 Service Strategy   27

4.1 Goals and objectives   29

4.2 Scope   29

4.3 Value creation   29

4.4 Key principles   30

4.5 Processes   32

4.6 Sample questions and answers   37

5 Service Design   39

5.1 Goals and objectives   41

5.2 Scope   41

5.3 Business value   41

5.4 Key principles   42

5.5 Processes   47

5.6 Sample questions and answers   59

6 Service Transition   61

6.1 Goals and objectives   63

6.2 Scope   63

6.3 Business value   65

6.4 Key principles   65

6.5 Processes   65

6.6 Sample questions and answers   77

7 Service Operation 79

7.1 Goals and objectives 81

7.2 Scope 81

7.3 Business value 81

7.4 Key principles 81

7.5 Processes 83

7.6 Functions 91

7.7 Sample questions and answers 97

8 Continual Service Improvement 101

8.1 Goals and objectives 103

8.2 Scope 103

8.3 Business value 103

8.4 Key principles 103

8.5 Processes 107

8.6 Sample questions and answers 111

9 Service Management Technology 113

9.1 Use of technology 115

9.2 Generic requirements 116

9.3 Service Automation 117

9.4 Service Analytics 118

9.5 Sample questions and answers 118

10 How it all fits together 121

10.1 Key links, inputs and outputs 123

10.2 Strategy implementation 124

10.3 Specialization and coordination 125

10.4 Monitoring and control 125

10.5 Continual Service Improvement 127

11 The examination and exam preparation 129

11.1 The examination 131

11.2 Exam preparation 131

12 Sample ITIL version 3 Foundation examination 133

12.1 Sample questions 135

12.2 Answers to sample questions 141

References and useful websites 145

Index 149

List of figures

Figure 1.1   The ITIL Qualification Scheme

Figure 2.1   Customer assets are the basis for defining value

Figure 2.2   Design constraints for a service

Figure 2 3   Service Management is the art of transforming resources into valuable services by exploiting the organization's capabilities

Figure 2.4   Value creation from service utilities and warranties

Figure 2.5   Differentiated offerings

Figure 2.6   Service composition

Figure 2.7   A basic process

Figure 2.8   The generic process elements

Figure 3.1   The ITIL Service Lifecycle

Figure 4.1   Elements of a Service Portfolio and Service Catalogue

Figure 4.2   Risk, risk analysis and risk management

Figure 4.3   Forming and formulating a Service Strategy

Figure 4.4   Service Portfolio process

Figure 5.1   The four Ps

Figure 5.2   Aligning new services to business requirements

Figure 5.3   The Service Portfolio and its contents

Figure 5.4   Architectural relationships

Figure 5.5   The Business Service Catalogue and the Technical Service Catalogue

Figure 5.6   Service Level Agreements (SLAs), Operational Level Agreements (OLAs) and Underpinning Contracts

Figure 5.7   The Service Level Management process

Figure 5.8   Supplier Management process

Figure 5.9   The Capacity Management process

Figure 5.10   The expanded Incident lifecycle

Figure 5.11   The Availability Management process

Figure 5.12   The Service Continuity Management process

Figure 5.13   Framework for managing IT security

Figure 6.1   The scope of Service Transition

Figure 6.2   The Service V-model

Figure 6.3   Example of a logical configuration model

Figure 6.4   Example of a Service Knowledge Management System

Figure 6.5   The Service Asset and Configuration Management process

Figure 6.6   Example process flow for a Normal Change

Figure 6.7   Simplified example of release units for an IT service

Figure 6.8   Relationship between the Definitive Media Library and the Configuration Management Database

Figure 6.9   The Release and Deployment process: coordinating the deployment of service components

Figure 7.1   A key role for Service Operation is to achieve a balance between conflicting sets of priorities

Figure 7.2   Calculating the priority based on impact and urgency

Figure 7.3   Incident Management process flow

Figure 7.4   Local Service Desk

Figure 7.5   Centralized Service Desk

Figure 7.6   Virtual Service Desk

Figure 8.1   The Deming Cycle

Figure 8.2   Continual Service Improvement model

Figure 8.3   Why do we measure?

Figure 8.4   The DIKW (data, information, knowledge and wisdom) model

Figure 8.5   From vision to measurements

Figure 8.6   The 7-Step Improvement Process

Figure 9.1   Types of service technology encounters

Figure 10.1   The Service Portfolio spine: key links, inputs and outputs in the Service Lifecycle

Figure 10.2   Strategy implementation through the Service Lifecycle

Figure 10.3   Service Management processes are applied across the Service Lifecycle

Figure 10.4   Monitoring and control across the Service Lifecycle

Figure 10.5   Continual Service Improvement throughout the Service Lifecycle

List of tables

Table 2.1   Resources and capabilities are
             types of service assets

Table 2.2   Example RACI matrix

Table 4.1   Sample business case structure

OGC's foreword

I have never particularly enjoyed the experience of sitting an exam. The anxious build-up, hours spent poring over pages of lengthy text, the intense atmosphere of the examination room. I could go on but I'm sure that most of you have been there at some point in your lives.

The best you can hope for in such a situation is to be well prepared. Study aids are an essential part of this and attending an accredited training course will also provide learning support, often with case studies and examples that can bring the ITIL® framework to life.

I must confess that even as co-founder of the ITIL concept and leader in its early development, I would not delight in taking the Foundation exam. Over the years, the content has been further developed and expanded as it incorporates the latest identified best practices. The sheer scope and depth of the complete ITIL Service Management Practices framework can seem daunting as an examination subject.

This publication successfully presents the content in a simplified structure, ideal for learning and developing knowledge. Sadly it won't make you an overnight success in the world of Service Management, but it will certainly point you in the right direction.

The next step, of course, is to pass the examination. But hopefully it won't seem such a challenge once you've studied the pages of this publication.

Best of luck!

John Stewart
Director, Policy and Standards, OGC

Chief Examiner's foreword

As the practices of ITIL become further embedded in organizations and the global Service Management industry, the recognition of IT Service Management (ITSM) as a profession grows in acceptance.

The ITIL Qualification Scheme supports the quest for formal knowledge and certification, and these are recognized not only for the Service Management capabilities they engender in the workplace but also as building blocks for a career path and as a symbol of ITSM professionalism.

The ITIL Foundation certificate for Service Management is the first of those building blocks. This publication is intended to help individuals studying the ITIL Foundation curriculum and preparing for the exam.

As part of a larger series of official study aids supporting ITIL qualifications, this publication will help students to understand the basics of ITIL Service Management practices and join the growing ranks of recognized Service Management professionals.

Knowledge gained today is the opportunity of tomorrow.

Sharon Taylor
Chief Examiner, ITIL

The Official Accreditor's foreword

The updating of ITIL to this current version has resulted in
several new topics being interwoven into the well-known
processes and approaches many people are familiar
with. ITIL version 3 is documented fully in five volumes
– *Service Strategy; Service Design; Service Transition;
Service Operation*; and *Continual Service Improvement* –
which provide detailed advice and guidance for Service
Management professionals.

This book aims to help candidates prepare for their
Foundation examination. It has been reviewed on behalf
of APMG by Mark Flynn of Felix Maldo Ltd and Gary
Hodgkiss of PTS Consulting. It is an excellent companion
to course notes and other material provided by
accredited training companies.

This book is endorsed by APMG and has itself passed a
rigorous assessment process.

We wish you every success with your forthcoming exam
and hope you will make full use of the excellent guidance
offered here.

Richard Pharro
CEO, The APM Group Ltd

Acknowledgements

CHIEF ARCHITECT AND AUTHOR

Sharon Taylor (Aspect Group Inc)   Chief Architect

Christian F Nissen (ITILLIGENCE)   Author

CONTRIBUTORS

A number of people generously contributed their time and expertise to this official ITIL Foundation study aid publication. The author especially would like to thank:

- Rosemary Gurney (Wardown Consulting Ltd) for her huge effort in making the language readable and understandable in English.
- Lise Dall Eriksen (ITILLIGENCE) who checked that the study aid publication covers all the topics in the ITIL version 3 Foundation syllabus.
- A number of IT Service Management experts, trainers and examiners including Lars Zobbe Mortensen (Zobbe Consult & Zoftware), Signe-Marie Hernes Bjerke (DNV), Thomas Fejfer (ITILLIGENCE), Katsushi Yaginuma (ITpreneurs), Majid Iqbal (Carnegie Mellon University), Ivor Macfarlane (IBM), Shirley Lacy (ConnectSphere) and Gary Case (Pink Elephant) for their comments and advice regarding the drafts produced in the development cycle.
- Bente Skøtt (OK Gasoline) who read and commented on the final draft as a representative for the target audience of the publication.
- Andrew Bates and Janine Eves from TSO who have been very supportive in answering questions and providing material and information during the development of the publication.

The ITIL
Qualification
Scheme

1

1 The ITIL Qualification Scheme: professional qualifications for ITIL practices for Service Management

The ITIL Service Management Practices are a consistent and comprehensive documentation of best practice for IT Service Management. Used by many hundreds of organizations around the world, a whole ITIL philosophy has grown up around the guidance contained within the ITIL publications and the supporting professional qualifications scheme.

The ITIL Service Management qualifications scheme supports ITIL practices to enable organizations to put their staff through approved training courses to gain practice knowledge and a recognized qualification. This has grown to become the international standard for IT Service Management in providing a common language and set of practices for use throughout the world.

The official ITIL Qualification Scheme is the only training and qualifications scheme leading to official ITIL qualifications in IT Service Management.

1.1 THREE LEVELS OF QUALIFICATION

The ITIL Qualification Scheme introduces a learning system that enables an individual to gain credits for all ITIL courses that can be applied toward a recognized professional achievement (Figure 1.1). Once candidates

Figure 1.1 The ITIL Qualification Scheme

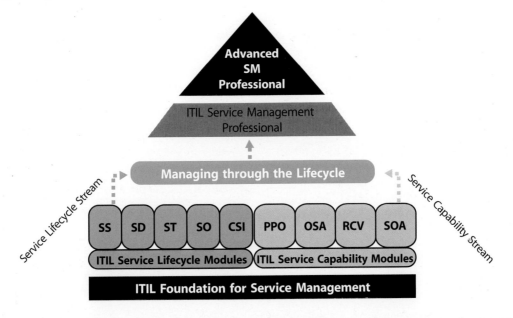

have accumulated a sufficient number of credits they can be awarded the ITIL Service Management Professional (ISMP[1]) standing in IT Service Management.

There are three levels within the new scheme, namely:

- Foundation level
- Intermediate (Service Lifecycle and Capability) level
- Advanced Professional level.

To achieve the ITIL ISMP certificate, candidates must achieve a minimum number of certification credits, two of which can be gained at the Foundation level. Each certification module in the scheme is awarded a credit value that contributes to the ISMP certificate.

1.1.1 ITIL Foundation certificate in IT Service Management

The Foundation level focuses on knowledge and comprehension to provide a good grounding in the key concepts, principles and processes of ITIL.

The learning objectives and competencies are focused on an understanding of the overall linkages between the stages in the lifecycle, the processes used and their contribution to Service Management practices.

More details of the ITIL Foundation certificate in IT Service Management can be found in Section 1.3.

1.1.2 ITIL Intermediate qualification certificates in IT Service Management

The ITIL Intermediate qualification certificates in IT Service Management are free-standing qualifications, but they also form a number of modules that lead to the ISMP certificate. The purpose of the certificates is to impart and test detailed knowledge about the contents of parts of the ITIL core publications.

The Intermediate qualifications are grouped in two sets or streams:

1 The Service Lifecycle series is focused on each stage of the lifecycle and syllabuses are matched to each of the five core practice areas. An examination is given for each module.
2 The Service Capability series is focused on role-based clusters in a modular set, each with an examination.

1.1.2.1 Service Lifecycle

The intermediate Service Lifecycle stream is built around the five ITIL core publications:

- Service Strategy (SS)
- Service Design (SD)
- Service Transition (ST)
- Service Operation (SO)
- Continual Service Improvement (CSI).

1.1.2.2 Service Capability

The intermediate Service Capability stream is built around four clusters:

- Operational Support and Analysis (OSA)
- Service Offerings and Agreements (SOA)
- Planning, Protection and Optimization (PPO)
- Release, Control and Validation (RCV).

Both intermediate streams assess an individual's comprehension and application of the concepts of ITIL.

Candidates are able to take units from either of the intermediate streams. These units give them credits towards an ITIL Service Management Professional (ISMP) certificate. Managing through the Lifecycle – a final intermediate course module – brings together the full essence of the lifecycle approach to Service Management.

---

1 ITIL Service Management Professional (ISMP) is a working title until the full scheme has been finalized by the ITIL Qualifications Board.

1.1.3 ITIL Service Management Professional certificate

Once a candidate has gained the required number of credits through their education and has successfully passed the required examinations at the Foundation and Intermediate levels, they will be awarded the ISMP certificate. No further examination or course is required to gain the ISMP certificate.

1.1.4 ITIL Advanced IT Service Management Professional

The ITIL Advanced Service Management Professional certificate in IT Service Management will assess an individual's ability to apply and analyse the ITIL concepts in new areas. This higher diploma had not been developed when this publication was released.

Details of the various learning options, certifications and combinations can be found on the ITIL Qualification Scheme website: http://www.itil-officialsite.com/Qualifications

1.2 QUALIFICATIONS BODIES

This section outlines the roles of the organizations within the official ITIL Qualification Scheme. Candidates should ensure that when buying ITIL training, it is acquired from an ITIL-accredited organization.

1.2.1 OGC

ITIL was originally developed by the UK government organization CCTA (Central Computer and Telecommunications Agency), which later became known as Office of Government Commerce (OGC), an office of HM Treasury.

OGC has established collaborative partnerships with two organizations to provide support for their ITIL portfolio. As the official accreditor, the APM Group (APMG) provides accreditation services related to examination institutes and training providers, and is responsible for the Qualification Scheme. The Stationery Office (TSO) is the official publisher of all official ITIL Service Management Practices framework publications, including this one.

OGC retains the rights to all intellectual property, copyright and trademarks relating to ITIL. Its predominant role in the official scheme is one of stewardship of the ITIL Service Management Practices framework content and qualifications. APMG chairs the Qualifications Board (the steering committee made up of representatives from the community who make decisions about qualifications policy) and ensure decisions made are to the benefit of both the practice and users alike.

1.2.2 APMG

APMG is an international professional accreditation and certification body which is accredited to international standards by UKAS (United Kingdom Accreditation Service). This proves the effectiveness, impartiality and quality of APMG's administration services. In 2006, APMG became OGC's official accreditor for ITIL and is now responsible for the monitoring and promotion of the official scheme for training, consulting and qualifications.

Within its role as the official ITIL accreditor, APMG is responsible for setting the standards and syllabuses throughout the market which any delivering Examination Institute must adhere to as well as creating, maintaining and delivering the ITIL qualifications itself.

APMG is also responsible for the accreditation, monitoring and surveillance of any Examination Institute applying to the official scheme to run ITIL qualifications and accredit training organizations.

1.2.3 Examination Institutes

APMG as the official accreditor is authorized to license other Examination Institutes to administer ITIL qualifications and accreditation activities.

Examination Institutes are allowed to complete the following activities:

- approve training organizations
- administer examinations via those organizations they have approved.

The current Examination Institutes are:

- Examination Institute for Information Science – EXIN
- Information Systems Examination Board – ISEB
- APM Group – APMG
- Loyalist Certification Services – LCS
- IT Dansk – ITD.

1.2.4 Accredited Training Organizations

Accredited Training Organizations (ATOs) are companies which have been assessed and approved by an Examination Institute to run officially accredited training courses and administer examinations in ITIL.

These accredited organizations must submit:

- their quality management systems, detailing their process for administration of the training courses and examinations
- the course material they utilize during training ITIL candidates for the examinations
- their trainers for assessment by an Examination Institute.

Following approval by an Examination Institute, ATOs are granted a licence by APMG as the official accreditor to use the relevant OGC-owned intellectual property rights and trademarks relating to ITIL.

1.2.5 *it*SMF International

The IT Service Management Forum (*it*SMF) is the not-for-profit international community for IT Service Management professionals, with over 40 chapters worldwide and a coordinating organization – *it*SMF International. The chapters provide local support to those individuals and organizations using and implementing ITIL.

*it*SMF is recognized as an integral part of the ITIL community and as such is a collaborative partner to the ITIL official scheme and participates on the Qualifications Board.

1.3 THE ITIL FOUNDATION CERTIFICATE IN IT SERVICE MANAGEMENT

1.3.1 Purpose

The purpose of the ITIL Foundation certificate in IT Service Management is to certify that the candidate has gained knowledge of the ITIL terminology, structure and basic concepts and has comprehended the core principles of ITIL practices for Service Management.

The ITIL Foundation certificate in IT Service Management is not intended to enable the holders of the certificate to apply the ITIL practices for Service Management without further guidance.

1.3.2 Target group

The target group of the ITIL Foundation certificate in IT Service Management is drawn from:

- individuals who require a basic understanding of the ITIL framework and how it may be used to enhance the quality of IT Service Management within an organization

- IT professionals who are working within an organization that has adopted and adapted ITIL, who need to be informed about and thereafter contribute to an ongoing Service Improvement Programme.

1.3.3 Prerequisites

There are no formal criteria or prerequisites for candidates wishing to attend an accredited ITIL Foundation course, though some familiarity with IT terminology and an appreciation of their own business environment is strongly recommended.

1.3.4 Learning objectives

The learning objectives of the ITIL Foundation certification in IT Service Management are to enable the candidate to:

- define service and explain the concept of Service Management as a practice
- understand the Service Lifecycle and explain the objectives and business value for each phase in the lifecycle
- define some of the key terminology and explain the key concepts of Service Management
- comprehend and account for the key principles and models of Service Management and to balance some of the opposing forces within Service Management
- understand how the Service Management processes contribute to the Service Lifecycle, to explain the high-level objectives, scope, basic concepts, activities, key metrics, roles and challenges for five of the core processes and to state the objectives, some of the basic concepts and roles for 15 of the remaining processes

- explain the role, objectives, organizational structures, staffing and metrics of the Service Desk function and to state the role, objectives and overlap of three other functions
- account for the role and to be aware of the responsibilities of some of the key roles in Service Management and to recognize a number of the remaining roles described in other learning units
- list some generic requirements for an integrated set of Service Management technologies and understand how service automation assists with integrating Service Management processes
- explain the ITIL Qualification Scheme.

1.3.5 Reference

The full syllabus with detailed descriptions of each of the learning objectives can be downloaded from the ITIL website: http://www.itil-officialsite.com

1.4 ABOUT THIS PUBLICATION

The content of this publication is based on the syllabus for the ITIL Foundation certificate in IT Service Management.

This publication is therefore neither an introduction to ITIL nor a brief summary of the ITIL core publications. Rather, it is a study aid to support the acquisition of knowledge and skills required to achieve the ITIL Foundation certificate in IT Service Management.

One of the Foundation learning objectives is to understand the common terminology used within ITIL. As such, readers may find it useful to access the official ITIL glossary of terms and definitions (see http://www.best-management-practice.com and navigate to 'Glossaries and Acronyms').

The structure of the publication does not strictly follow the order of the syllabus. Instead it is structured with ease of learning in mind. Basic concepts are introduced in Chapters 2 and 3 ('Service Management as a Practice' and 'The Service Lifecycle') to form the basis for the concepts, principles and practices that are introduced in the subsequent five chapters, each representing a core publication. Each of the five core chapters is identically structured to help the acquisition of the covered concepts, principles and concepts. The two subsequent chapters ('Service Management Technology' and 'How it all fits together') contain transverse topics.

At the end of each chapter a number of sample test questions are presented to enable the reader to practise the content of the chapter. The number of questions in each chapter corresponds to the typical distribution of questions in an exam.

Hopefully you will find IT Service Management enjoyable and you will acquire the new knowledge and skills necessary for achieving the ITIL Foundation certificate in IT Service Management.

Service Management as a practice

2

2 Service Management as a practice

Service Management is a professional practice supported by an extensive body of knowledge, experience and skills.

2.1 SERVICES

A service facilitates outcomes by enhancing performance and by reducing the influence of constraints. The result is an increase in business outcomes.

> **Definition**
> A service is a means of delivering value to customers by facilitating the outcomes customers want to achieve without the ownership of specific costs and risks.

Outcomes are possible from the performance of tasks and are limited by the presence of constraints.

Business outcomes and performance of customer assets are the basis for the value created by services (Figure 2.1).

Customer needs translate into attributes of a service, which in turn determine a set of design constraints (Figure 2.2).

Design constraints are of various types. Their combined effect is to define a solution space for the service that is feasible in terms of meeting customer needs, enhancing performance and reducing the influence of constraints.

Figure 2.1 Customer assets are the basis for defining value

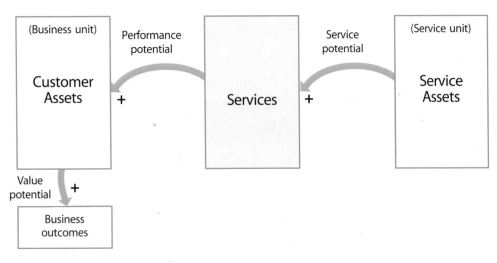

Figure 2.2 Design constraints for a service

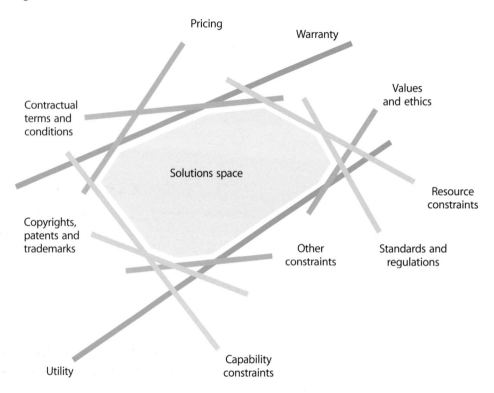

2.2 SERVICE MANAGEMENT

> **Definition**
> Service Management is a set of specialized organizational capabilities for providing value to customers in the form of services.

The capabilities represent a service organization's capacity, competency and confidence for action. The capabilities take the form of *functions* and *processes* for managing services.

Figure 2.3 Service Management is the art of transforming resources into valuable services by exploiting the organization's capabilities

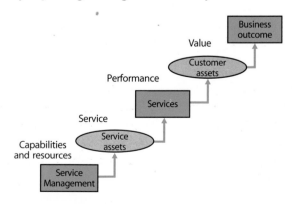

The act of transforming resources (Figure 2.3) into valuable services is at the core of Service Management. Without the capabilities, a service organization is merely a bundle of useless *resources*.

Service Management, however, is more than just a set of capabilities. It is also a professional *practice* supported by an extensive body of knowledge, experience and skills. A global community of individuals and organizations fosters its growth and maturity.

2.3 RESOURCES AND CAPABILITIES

Resources and capabilities are types of *service assets*. Organizations use them to create value in the form of goods and services.

> **Definition**
> Resource is a generic term that includes IT infrastructure, people, money or anything else that might help to deliver an IT service. Resources are considered to be assets of an organization.

Resources are direct inputs for production.

Capabilities such as management, organization, people and knowledge are used to transform resources into valuable services.

> **Definition**
> Capability is the ability of a service organization, person, process, application, Configuration Item or IT service to carry out an activity. Capabilities are intangible assets of an organization.

Capabilities represent an organization's ability to coordinate, control and deploy resources to produce value. They are typically experience driven, knowledge intensive, information based and firmly embedded within an organization's people, systems, processes and technologies (see Table 2.1).

Table 2.1 Resources and capabilities are types of service assets

Resources	Capabilities
Financial capital	Management
Infrastructure	Organization
Applications	Processes
Information	Knowledge
People	

2.4 UTILITY AND WARRANTY

From the customer's perspective, the business value of a service is created by the combination of two elements (see Figure 2.4):

- Utility: what the customer gets – or fitness for purpose
- Warranty: how it is delivered – or fitness for use.

> **Definition**
> Utility is the functionality offered by a product or service from the customer's perspective.

Utility increases the *performance average*.

> **Definition**
> Warranty is a promise or guarantee that a product or service will meet its agreed requirements. This may be a formal agreement such as a Service Level Agreement or Contract, or it may be a marketing message or brand image.

Three characteristics of warranty are:

- it is provided in terms of the *availability* and *capacity* of services
- it ensures that customer assets *continue* to receive *utility*, even if at degraded service levels, through major disruptions or disasters

■ it ensures security for the value creating potential of customer assets.

Warranty reduces the *performance variation*.

Customers cannot benefit from something that is fit for purpose but not fit for use, and vice versa. It is useful to separate the logic of utility from the logic of warranty for the purpose of design, development and improvement.

2.5 SERVICE PACKAGES

Core services deliver the basic outcomes desired by the customer. They represent the value that the customer wants and for which they are willing to pay.

Supporting services either enable or enhance the value of a service. Enabling services are basic factors that qualify the provider for an opportunity to serve and enhancing services are excitement factors for differentiation.

2.5.1 Service Package

Definition
A Service Package is a detailed description of an IT service that is available to be delivered to customers. A Service Package includes one or more core services and supporting services, as well as a Service Level Package.

Bundling of Core Service Packages with enabling and enhancing Service Packages enables differentiated offerings (Figure 2.5).

Some supporting services such as Service Desk, typically bundled with most Service Packages, can also be offered on their own.

Services Packages come with one or more Service Level Packages.

Figure 2.4 Value creation from service utilities and warranties

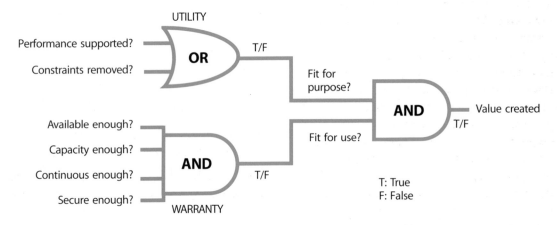

Figure 2.5 Differentiated offerings

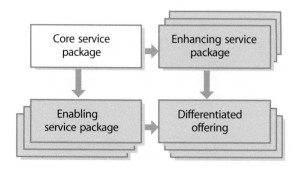

2.5.2 Service composition

All the components of the service and their inter-relationships have to be considered, ensuring that the services delivered meet new and evolving business needs. The various components (Figure 2.6) are:

- **Business process:** The process that defines the functional needs of the service being provided, e.g. telesales, invoicing, orders, credit checking.
- **Service:** The service itself that is being delivered to customers and business by the service provider, e.g. e-mail, billing.
- **Service Level Agreements (SLAs)/Service Level Requirements (SLRs):** The documents agreed with the customer that specify the level, scope and quality of service to be provided.
- **Infrastructure:** All of the IT equipment necessary to deliver the service to customers and users, including servers, network circuits, switches, personal computers (PCs), telephones.
- **Environment:** The environment required to secure and operate the infrastructure, e.g. data centres, power, air conditioning.
- **Data:** The data necessary to support the service and provide the information required by the business processes, e.g. customer records, accounts ledger.

- **Applications:** All of the software applications required to manipulate the data and provide the functional requirements of the business processes, e.g. Enterprise Resource Management (ERM), Financial, Customer Relationship Management (CRM).
- **Support services:** Any services that are necessary to support the operation of the delivered service, e.g. a shared service, a managed network service.
- **Operational Level Agreements (OLAs) and contracts:** Any underpinning agreements necessary to deliver the quality of service agreed within the SLA.
- **Support teams:** Any internal support teams providing second-line and third-line support for any of the components required to provide the service.
- **Suppliers:** Any external third parties necessary to provide third-line and fourth-line support for any of the components required to provide the service.

2.6 PROCESSES, FUNCTIONS AND ROLES

2.6.1 Processes

2.6.1.1 Process

Definition

A process is a set of coordinated activities combining and implementing resources and capabilities in order to produce an outcome, which, directly or indirectly, creates value for an external customer or stakeholder.

A process takes one or more defined inputs and turns them into defined outputs.

A process may include any of the roles, responsibilities, tools and management controls required to reliably deliver the outputs.

A process may define policies, standards, guidelines, activities and work instructions if they are needed.

Figure 2.6 Service composition

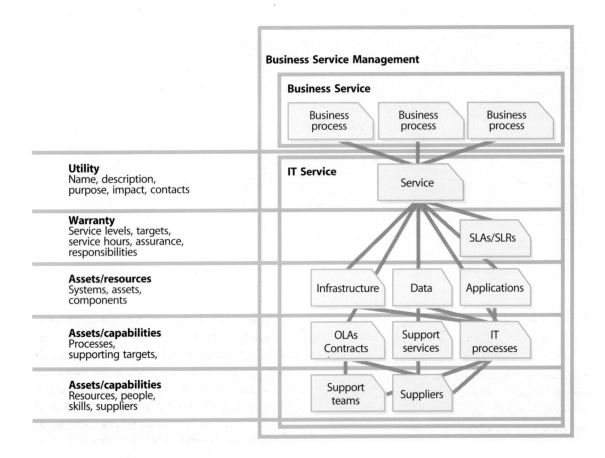

Business Service Management

Business Service

Business process · Business process · Business process

Utility
Name, description,
purpose, impact, contacts

IT Service
Service

Warranty
Service levels, targets,
service hours, assurance,
responsibilities

SLAs/SLRs

Assets/resources
Systems, assets,
components

Infrastructure · Data · Applications

Assets/capabilities
Processes,
supporting targets,

OLAs Contracts · Support services · IT processes

Assets/capabilities
Resources, people,
skills, suppliers

Support teams · Suppliers

Processes become strategic assets when they create competitive advantage and market differentiation.

2.6.1.2 Closed-loop systems

Process definitions describe actions, dependencies and sequence. Measuring and steering the activities increases effectiveness, and by adding norms to the process, it is possible to add quality measures to the output (Figure 2.7).

Processes are examples of closed-loop systems because they provide change and transformation towards a goal, and use feedback for self-reinforcing and self-corrective action. It is important to consider the entire process or how one process fits into another.

Figure 2.7 A basic process

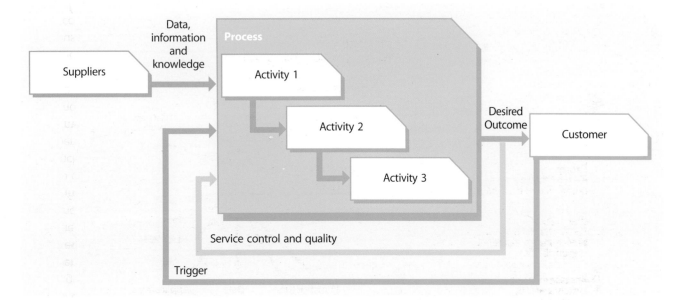

2.6.1.3 Process model

Processes, once defined, should be *documented* and *controlled*; once under control, they can be repeated and become manageable. Degrees of control over processes can be defined, and then process measurement and metrics can be built into the process to control and improve the process as illustrated in Figure 2.8.

The generic process elements (Figure 2.8) show that data enters the process, is processed and exits, and the outcome is measured and reviewed.

A process is organized around a set of *objectives*. The main outputs from the process should be driven by the objectives and should always include process *measurements* (metrics), *reports* and *process improvement*.

Each process should be owned by a Process Owner, who should be responsible for the process and its improvement and for ensuring that a process meets its objectives.

The *output* produced by a process has to conform to operational norms that are derived from business objectives. If products conform to the set norm, the process can be considered effective (because it can be repeated, measured and managed). If the activities are carried out with a minimum use of *resources*, the process can also be considered efficient. Process analysis, results and metrics should be incorporated in regular management reports and process improvements.

Documentation standards, processes and templates should be used to ensure that the processes are easily adopted throughout an organization.

Figure 2.8 The generic process elements

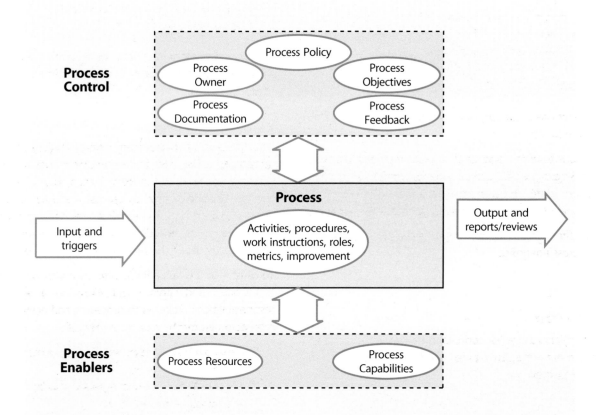

2.6.1.4 Process characteristics

Processes have the following characteristics:

- **Measurable** – Ability to measure the process in a relevant manner. It is performance driven. Managers want to measure cost, quality and other variables whereas practitioners are concerned with duration and productivity.
- **Specific results** – The reason a process exists is to deliver a specific result.

- **Customers** – Every process delivers its primary results to a customer or stakeholder. They may be internal or external to an organization but the process must meet their expectations.
- **Responds to a specific Event** – While a process may be ongoing or iterative, it should be traceable to a specific trigger.

2.6.2 Functions

Definition
A function is an organizational unit specialized to perform certain types of work and is responsible for specific outcomes. It is self-contained with capabilities and resources necessary for its performance and outcomes.

In smaller organizations, one person or group can perform multiple functions.

Functions tend to optimize their work methods locally to focus on assigned outcomes. Poor coordination between functions combined with an inward focus leads to functional silos that hinder cross-organizational cooperation.

Well-defined processes can improve productivity within and across functions.

2.6.3 Roles

2.6.3.1 Role

A role refers to a set of connected behaviours or actions that are performed by a person, team or group in a specific context.

Definition
A role is a set of responsibilities, activities and authorities granted to a person or team. A role is defined in a process.

One person or team may have multiple roles, for example the roles of Configuration Manager and Change Manager may be carried out by a single person.

2.6.3.2 RACI

Since processes and their component activities run through an entire organization, the individual activities should be mapped to the roles defined. The roles and activities are coordinated by process managers. Once detailed procedures and work instructions have been developed, an organization must map the defined roles and the activities of the process to its existing staff.

To assist with this task a RACI authority matrix (see Table 2.2) is often used within organizations indicating roles and responsibilities in relation to processes and activities. RACI is an acronym for the four main roles of:

- **Responsible** – the person or people responsible for getting the job done
- **Accountable** – only one person can be accountable for each task

Table 2.2 Example RACI matrix

	Director Service Management	Service Level Manager	Problem Manager	Security Manager	Procurement Manager
Activity 1	AR	C	I	I	C
Activity 2	A	R	C	C	C
Activity 3	I	A	R	I	C
Activity 4	I	A	R	I	
Activity 5	I	I	A	C	I

- **Consulted** – the people who are consulted and whose opinions are sought
- **Informed** – the people who are kept up to date on progress.

Occasionally, an expanded version of RACI, called RACI-VS, is used with two more roles as follows:

- **Verifies** – the person or group that checks whether the acceptance criteria have been met
- **Signs off** – the person who approves the verification decision and authorizes the product hand-off. This could be the accountable person.

The RACI chart (Table 2.2) shows the structure of RACI modelling with the activities down the left-hand side including the actions that need to be taken and decisions that must be made. Across the top, the chart lists the functional roles responsible for carrying out the initiative or playing a part in decision making.

2.6.4 Process Owner

A Process Owner is the role responsible for ensuring that their process is being performed according to the agreed and documented process, and that it is meeting the aims of the process definition.

Process ownership includes such responsibilities as:

- defining the process strategy
- defining appropriate policies and standards to be employed throughout the process
- assisting with and ultimately being responsible for the process design
- documenting and publicizing the process
- defining and reviewing the key performance indicators (KPIs) to evaluate the effectiveness and efficiency of the process and taking the required action
- improving the effectiveness and efficiency of the process

- communicating process information or changes as appropriate to ensure awareness
- providing input to the ongoing Service Improvement Programme
- addressing any issues with the running of the process
- ensuring all relevant staff have the required training in the process and are aware of their role in the process
- ensuring that the process, roles, responsibilities and documentation are regularly reviewed and audited
- interfacing with line management to ensure that the process receives the needed staff resources.

2.6.5 Service Owner

The Service Owner is accountable for a specific service within an organization, regardless of where the underpinning technology components, processes or professional capabilities reside.

Service ownership is as critical to Service Management as establishing ownership for processes, which crosses multiple vertical silos or departments.

The Service Owner:

- is Service Owner for a specified service
- understands the service (components etc.)
- acts as prime Customer contact for all service-related enquiries and issues
- ensures that the ongoing service delivery and support meet agreed customer requirements
- identifies opportunities for Service Improvements, discusses these with the customer and raises a Request for Change (RFC) for assessment if appropriate
- participates in negotiating SLAs and OLAs
- represents the service in Change Advisory Board (CAB) meetings

- liaises with the appropriate Process Owners throughout the Service Management lifecycle
- participates in internal service review meetings within IT and external service review meetings with the business
- is accountable for the delivery of the service.

2.7 GOOD PRACTICE

Organizations often benchmark themselves against peers and seek to close gaps in *capabilities*. One way to the close such gaps is the adoption of good practices.

Practice is a way of working or a way in which work must be done. Practices can include activities, processes, functions, standards and guidelines.

By good or best practice we mean proven activities or processes that have been successfully used by multiple organizations.

There are several sources for good practices including public frameworks, standards and the proprietary knowledge of organizations and individuals:

- Standards
- Industry practices
- Academic research
- Training and education
- Internal experience.

ITIL is an example of good practice. It is used by organizations worldwide to establish and improve capabilities in Service Management.

ISO/IEC 20000 provides a formal and universal standard for organizations seeking to have their Service Management capabilities audited and certified.

2.8 SAMPLE QUESTIONS AND ANSWERS

2.8.1 Questions

1 Which of the following does NOT represent a capability of a service organization?
  a Confidence for action
  b Customers
  c Capacity
  d Competency.

2 Which of the following characterizes a function?
  1 It is specialized to perform a certain type of work
  2 It is self-contained with capabilities and resources necessary for its performance
  3 It is responsible for specific outcomes
  4 It can be repeated and becomes manageable.
  a 1 only
  b 1 and 3 only
  c 1, 2 and 3 only
  d All of the above.

3 Which of the following are characteristics of a process?
  1 Measurable
  2 Responds to a specific Event
  3 Has customers
  4 Leads to specific results.
  a 1 only
  b 1 and 3 only
  c 1, 2 and 3 only
  d All of the above.

4 In the RACI authority matrix the letter 'C' stands for:
  a Classified
  b Configured
  c Consulted
  d Communication.

5 Which of the following activities is a Process Owner of a specific process responsible for?
   1 Documenting and publicizing the process
   2 Participating in negotiating Service Level Agreements
   3 Defining the process strategy
   4 Providing input to the ongoing Service Improvement Programme.
   a 1 only
   b 1 and 3 only
   c 1, 3 and 4 only
   d All of the above

6 The Service Owner is accountable for a specific service within an organization:
   a only if all underpinning resources and capabilities reside inside the organization
   b only if all underpinning resources, but not necessarily the capabilities, reside inside the organization
   c only if all underpinning capabilities, but not necessarily the resources, reside inside the organization
   d regardless of where the underpinning resources and capabilities reside.

2.8.2 Answers

1 b – The customers of an organization are not a capability.

2 c – Option 4 (It can be repeated and becomes manageable) is a characteristic of a process.

3 d – All the four options are process characteristics.

4 c – RACI is an acronym for 'Responsible', 'Accountable', 'Consulted' and 'Informed'.

5 c – Except for option 2, which is the responsibility for the Service Owner, the Service Level Manager etc., the rest of the activities form part of the responsibilities of the Process Owner.

6 d – The ownership is not affected by where the resources and capabilities reside.

The Service Lifecycle

3

3 The Service Lifecycle

The Service Lifecycle is iterative and multidimensional. It ensures that organizations are set up to leverage capabilities in one area for learning and for improvements in others.

3.1 THE ITIL SERVICE MANAGEMENT PRACTICES

The ITIL Service Management Practices framework has the following components:

- ITIL Core – best practice guidance applicable to all types of organization that provide services to a business
- ITIL Complementary Guidance – a complementary set of publications with guidance specific to industry sectors, organization types, operating models, and technology architectures. (This publication is an example of Complementary Guidance.)

The guidance in ITIL can be *adapted* for use in various business environments and organizational strategies.

The Complementary Guidance provides flexibility to adapt the core practices in a diverse range of environments. Practitioners can select Complementary Guidance as needed to provide traction for the core in a given business context, much like tyres are selected based on the type of automobile, purpose and road conditions.

3.2 THE SERVICE LIFECYCLE

The architecture of ITIL Service Management practices is based on a Service Lifecycle. Each volume of the core is represented in the Service Lifecycle (Figure 3.1). Service Design, Service Transition and Service Operation are progressive phases of the lifecycle and represent change and transformation. Service Strategy represents policies and objectives. Continual Service Improvement (CSI) represents learning and improvement.

Figure 3.1 The ITIL Service Lifecycle

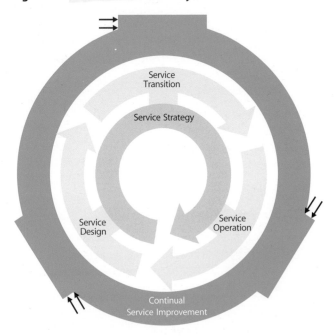

Service Strategy is the axis around which the lifecycle rotates. Service Design, Service Transition, and Service Operation implement strategy. CSI helps place improvement programmes based on strategic objectives.

Each publication addresses capabilities that have a direct impact on a Service Provider's performance.

3.2.1 Service Strategy

The *Service Strategy* volume provides guidance on how to design, develop and implement Service Management not only as an organizational capability but also as a strategic asset.

Topics covered in *Service Strategy* include the development of markets, both internal and external, service assets, Service Catalogue and implementation of strategy through the Service Lifecycle. Financial Management, Service Portfolio Management, organizational development and strategic risks are other major topics.

3.2.2 Service Design

The *Service Design* volume provides guidance for the design and development of services and processes. It covers design principles and methods for converting strategic objectives into portfolios of services and service assets.

3.2.3 Service Transition

The *Service Transition* volume provides guidance for the development and improvement of capabilities for transitioning new and changed services into operations.

Service Transition provides guidance on how the requirements of Service Strategy encoded in Service Design are effectively realized in Service Operation while controlling the risks of failure and disruption. The publication combines practices in Release Management, programme management and risk management.

3.2.4 Service Operation

The *Service Operation* volume embodies practices in the management of Service Operation. It includes guidance on achieving effectiveness and efficiency in the delivery and support of services to ensure value for the customer and the Service Provider.

3.2.5 Continual Service Improvement

The *Continual Service Improvement* volume provides instrumental guidance in creating and maintaining value for customers through better design, introduction and operation of services. It combines principles, practices and methods from quality management, Change Management and capability improvement.

3.3 SAMPLE QUESTION AND ANSWER

3.3.1 Question

1 Which of the following does NOT represent a stage in the Service Lifecycle?
 - a Continual Service Improvement
 - b Service Operation
 - c Service Architecture
 - d Service Strategy.

3.3.2 Answer

1 c – Options (a), (b) and (d) are all stages of the lifecycle. Two other lifecycle stages not mentioned in the question are 'Service Design' and 'Service Transition'.

Service Strategy

4 Service Strategy

Guidance on how to design, develop and implement Service Management not only as an organizational capability but as a strategic asset.

Guidance on how to set objectives and expectations of performance towards serving customers and market spaces and to identify, select and prioritize opportunities.

4.1 GOALS AND OBJECTIVES

The main goal is to encourage Service Providers to think about *why* something is to be done before thinking of how – that is, to think and act in a strategic manner.

The objectives of Service Strategy are to answer questions such as:

- What services should we offer and to whom?
- How do we differentiate ourselves from competing alternatives?
- How do we truly create value for our customers and stakeholders?
- How can we make a case for strategic investments?
- How can Financial Management provide visibility and control over value creation?
- How should we define service quality?
- How do we choose between different paths for improving service quality?
- How do we efficiently allocate resources across a portfolio of services?
- How do we resolve conflicting demands for shared resources?

4.2 SCOPE

The scope of Service Strategy includes:

- development of markets, internal and external
- service assets
- Service Catalogue
- implementation of strategy
- Financial Management, Demand Management, Service Portfolio Management and organizational development
- strategic risks.

4.3 VALUE CREATION

Resources and capabilities are types of asset. Organizations use them to *create value* in the form of goods and services.

Capabilities are developed over time. The development of capabilities is enhanced by the experience gained from the number and variety of customers, market spaces, contracts and services. Experience is similarly enriched from solving problems, handling situations, managing risks and analysing failures.

Capabilities by themselves cannot produce value without *resources*. The productive capacity of a Service Provider is dependent on the resources under their control. Capabilities are used to develop, deploy and coordinate this productive capacity.

4.4 KEY PRINCIPLES

4.4.1 Service Portfolio

The Service Portfolio is the most critical management system used to support all processes and describes a provider's services in terms of business value. It articulates business needs and the provider's response to those needs.

> **Definition**
> The Service Portfolio is the complete set of services that are managed by a Service Provider.

The portfolio also includes third-party services, which are an integral part of service offerings to customers. Some third-party services are visible to the customers whereas others are not.

By acting as the basis of a decision framework, a Service Portfolio either clarifies or helps to clarify the following strategic questions:

- Why should a customer buy these services?
- Why should they buy these services from us?
- What are the pricing or chargeback models?
- What are our strengths and weaknesses, priorities and risks?
- How should our resources and capabilities be allocated?

The portfolio management approach helps managers prioritize investments and improve the allocation of resources. Changes to portfolios are governed by policies and procedures.

4.4.2 Service Catalogue

The Service Catalogue is a database or structured document with information about all live IT services, including those available for deployment and operation. The Service Catalogue is the only part of the Service Portfolio visible to current or prospective customers, and it is used to support the sale and delivery of IT services.

Figure 4.1 Elements of a Service Portfolio and Service Catalogue

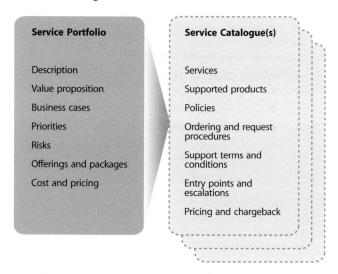

The Service Catalogue includes information about deliverables, prices, contact points, ordering and request processes (Figure 4.1).

It is in the Service Catalogue that services are decomposed into components; it is where assets, processes and systems are introduced with entry points and terms for their use and provisioning. As providers may have many customers or serve many businesses, there may be multiple Service Catalogues chartered from the Service Portfolio. In other words a Service Catalogue is an expression of the provider's operational capability within the context of a customer or market space.

4.4.3 Business case

A business case is a decision-support and planning tool that projects the likely consequences of a business action. The consequences can take on qualitative and quantitative dimensions.

Definition
A business case is a justification for a significant item of expenditure. It includes information about costs, benefits, options, issues, risks and possible problems.

The business case should articulate the reason for undertaking a service or process improvement initiative (see Table 4.1). As far as possible, data and evidence should be provided relating to the costs and expected benefits of undertaking process improvement.

Table 4.1 Sample business case structure

Business case structure
A. Introduction Presents the business objectives addressed by the service
B. Methods and assumptions Defines the boundaries of the business case, such as time period, whose costs and whose benefits
C. Business impacts The financial and non-financial business case results
D. Risks and contingencies The probability that alternative results will emerge
E. Recommendations Specific actions recommended

In developing a business case, the focus should not only be on Return on Investment (ROI) but also on the business value that Service Improvement brings to an organization and its customers (Value on Investment – VOI).

4.4.4 Management of risk

4.4.4.1 Risk

Definition
Risk is a possible Event that could cause harm or loss, or affect the ability to achieve objectives.

A risk is measured by the probability of a Threat, the vulnerability of the asset to that Threat, and the impact if it occurred (Figure 4.2).

4.4.4.2 Risk analysis

Risk analysis is concerned with identifying risks so that the organization can make appropriate decisions and manage risk appropriately. Risk analysis involves the identification and assessment of the level of the risks calculated from the assessed *values of assets* and the assessed *levels of threats* to, and *vulnerabilities* of, those assets.

4.4.4.3 Risk management

Management of risk involves having processes in place to monitor risks, access to reliable and up-to-date information about risks, the right balance of control in place to deal with those risks, and decision-making processes supported by a framework of risk analysis and evaluation.

Risk management also involves the identification, selection and adoption of countermeasures justified by the identified risks.

Figure 4.2 Risk, risk analysis and risk management

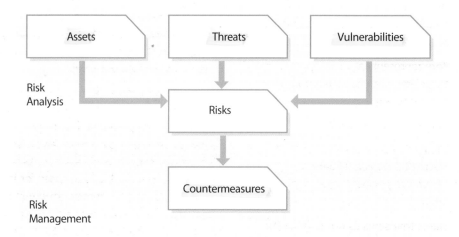

4.5 PROCESSES

4.5.1 Strategy generation

The strategy generation process takes in four activities:

1 define the market
2 develop the offerings
3 develop strategic assets
4 prepare for execution.

4.5.1.1 Define the market

Services and strategy

Organizations have an interest in strategy within the context of Service Management from two distinct but related perspectives. There are *strategies for services* and there are *services for strategies*:

- From one perspective, strategies are developed for services offered. Providers differentiate their services from competing alternatives available to customers.
- From the other perspective, Service Management is a competence for offering services as part of a business strategy.

Understand the customer

The performance of customer assets should be a primary concern of Service Management because without customer assets there is no basis for defining the value of service.

Some services increase the performance of customer assets, some services maintain performance and yet others restore performance following adverse events.

Understand the opportunities

Customer outcomes that are not well supported represent opportunities for services to be offered as solutions.

An outcome-based definition of services ensures that Service Management is planned and executed entirely from the perspective of what is valuable to the customer. Such an approach ensures that services not only create value for customers but also capture value for the Service Provider.

4.5.1.2 Develop offerings

Define the market space

A market space is defined by a set of business outcomes that customers desire.

A market space therefore represents a set of opportunities for Service Providers to deliver value to a customer's business through one or more services.

Outcome-based definition of services

An outcome-based definition of services ensures that managers plan and execute all aspects of Service Management entirely from the perspective of what is valuable to the customer.

Such an approach ensures that services not only create value for customers but also capture value for the Service Provider.

Service Portfolio, Pipeline and Catalogue

The Service Portfolio represents the commitments and investments made by a Service Provider across all customers and market spaces. It represents present contractual commitments, new service development, and ongoing Service Improvement Programmes initiated by CSI.

The Service Portfolio is divided into three phases:

- Service Catalogue
- Service Pipeline
- Retired Services.

Approval from Service Transition is necessary to add or to remove services from the Service Catalogue.

4.5.1.3 Develop strategic assets

Service Providers should treat Service Management as a strategic asset.

Increase the service potential

The *capabilities* and *resources* (service assets) of a service provider represent the service potential or the productive capacity available to customers through a set of services. Projects that develop or improve capabilities and resources increase the service potential.

Through Configuration Management, all service assets should be tagged with the name of the services to which they add service potential. This helps making decisions related to service improvement and asset management. Clear relationships make it easier to ascertain the impact of changes, to make business cases for investments in service assets, and to identify opportunities for scale and scope economies. Configuration Management identifies critical service assets across the Service Portfolio for a given customer or market space.

Increase performance potential

The services offered by a Service Provider represent the potential to increase the performance of customer assets. Without this potential there is no justification for customers to procure the services.

The performance potential of services is increased primarily by having the right mix of services to offer to customers.

Manage Demand, Capacity and Cost

When services are effective in increasing the performance potential of customer assets there is an increase in the demand for the services.

As the maturity of Service Management increases, it is possible to deliver higher levels of utility and warranty without a proportional increase in costs.

Figure 4.3 Forming and formulating a Service Strategy

Figure 4.3 Forming and formulating a Service Strategy

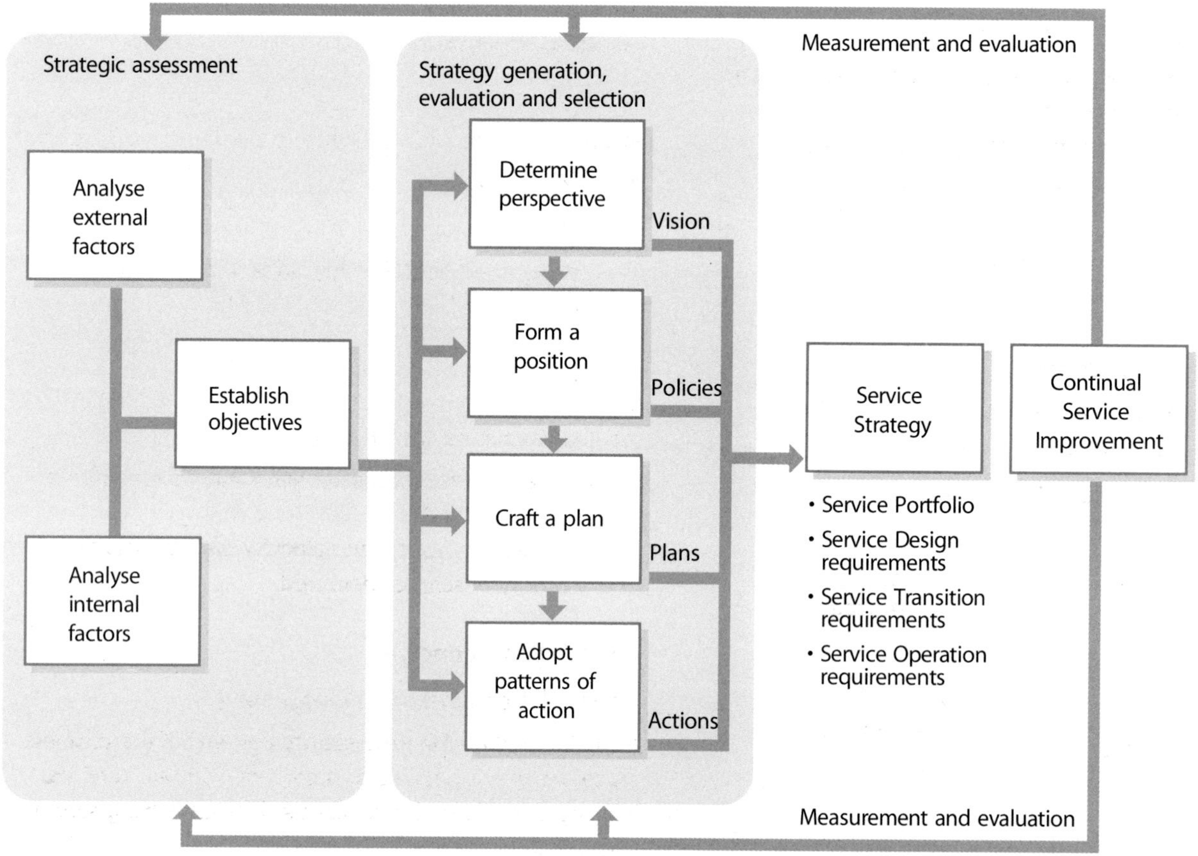

4.5.1.4 Prepare for execution

Service Strategies must be formed and formulated (Figure 4.3).

Analyse internal and external factors

In crafting a Service Strategy, a provider should first take a careful look at what it already does. It is likely there already exists a core of differentiation.

Set objectives

Objectives represent the results expected from pursuing strategies, while strategies represent the actions to be taken to accomplish objectives. Clear objectives provide for consistent decision making, minimizing later conflicts.

Prioritize investments – strategy generation, evaluation and selection

One common problem Service Providers have is prioritizing investments and managerial attention on the right set of opportunities. Service Portfolios should be extended to support such areas of opportunity. This typically means that there is a need for services to provide certain levels of utility and warranty.

4.5.2 Service Portfolio Management

4.5.2.1 Goals and objectives

- To maximize return on the Service Portfolio at an acceptable risk level.
- To make appropriate changes to the Service Portfolio when conditions change.

The value of a Service Portfolio strategy is demonstrated through its ability to anticipate change while maintaining traceability to strategy and planning.

4.5.2.2 Basic concepts

The Service Portfolio Management process includes the following work activities (Figure 4.4).

Figure 4.4 Service Portolio process

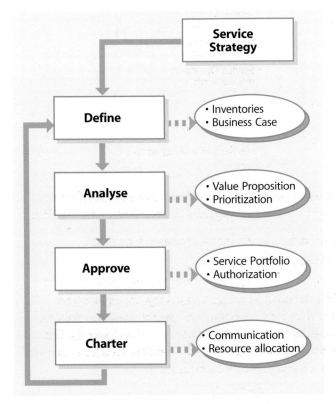

Define

Define inventory services, ensure business cases and validate portfolio data.

Analyse

Maximize portfolio value, align, and prioritize and balance supply and demand.

Approve

Finalize proposed portfolio, authorize services and resources.

4.5.3 Demand Management

4.5.3.1 Goals and objectives

- To avoid excess capacity-generating costs without creating value.
- To prevent insufficient capacity that impacts on the quality of services delivered.

4.5.3.2 Basic concepts

Activity-based Demand Management

Analysing and tracking the activity patterns of the business process makes it possible to predict demand for services. It is also possible to predict demand for underlying service assets that support those services.

Patterns of Business Activity

Business activities drive demand for services. Customer assets such as people, processes and applications generate Patterns of Business Activity.

> **Definition**
> Pattern of Business Activity is a workload profile of one or more business activities. Patterns of Business Activity are used to help the IT Service Provider understand and plan for different levels of business activity.

Differentiated offerings and service levels

Service Level Packages are effective in developing Service Packages for providing value to a segment of users with utility and warranty appropriate to their needs in a cost-effective way. Service Level Packages are combined with Core Service Packages to build a Service Catalogue with segmentation.

4.5.4 Financial Management

4.5.4.1 Goals and objectives

- To provide operational visibility, insight and superior decision making.
- To provide the business and IT with the quantification, in financial terms, of the value of IT services, the value of the assets underlying the provisioning of those services, and the qualification of operational forecasting.
- To ensure proper funding for the delivery and consumption of services.

4.5.4.2 Basic concepts

Financial Management feeds critical decisions and activities such as:

- service valuation
- calculating and assigning a monetary value to a service or service component.

The service value elements of utility and warranty require translation of their value to an actual monetary figure.

Demand modelling

Financial demand modelling focuses on identifying the total cost of utilization to the customer and predicting the financial implications of future service demand.

Service Provisioning Optimization

Financial Management provides key inputs for Service Provisioning Optimization (SPO). SPO examines the financial inputs and constraints of service components or delivery models to determine if alternatives should be explored relating to how a service can be provisioned differently to make it more competitive in terms of cost or quality.

Planning and budgeting

Planning provides financial translation and qualification of expected future demand for IT services.

Service Investment Analysis

The objective of Service Investment Analysis is to derive a value indication for the total lifecycle of a service based on the *value* received and costs incurred during the lifecycle of the service.

Accounting

The functions and accounting characteristics are typically:

- service recording – the assignment of a cost entry to the appropriate service
- cost types – these are higher-level expense categories such as hardware, software, resource and administration
- cost classifications – there are also classifications within services that designate the end purpose of the cost. These include classifications such as:
  - capital/operational
  - direct/indirect
  - fixed/variable
  - cost units.

Compliance

Compliance relates to the ability to demonstrate that proper and consistent accounting methods and/or practices are being employed.

4.6 SAMPLE QUESTIONS AND ANSWERS

4.6.1 Questions

1 A risk is measured by:
    1 the probability of a threat
    2 the vulnerability of the asset to a threat
    3 the countermeasures put in place
    4 the impact if a threat occurs.
  a 1 only
  b 2 and 4 only
  c 1, 2 and 4 only
  d All of the above.

2 The value of a service is determined by:
    1 Preferences
    2 Practice
    3 Perceptions
    4 Business outcome.
  a 1 only
  b 1 and 3 only
  c 1, 3 and 4 only
  d All of the above.

3 What are the MAIN activities in the Service Strategy management process?
    1 Define the market
    2 Develop the offerings
    3 Develop strategic assets
    4 Prepare for execution.
  a 4 only
  b 2 and 3 only
  c 1, 2 and 3 only
  d All of the above.

4 Which of the following activities is NOT an activity in the Financial Management process?
  a Service devaluation
  b Service Portfolio Management
  c Service Investment Analysis
  d Compliance.

5 Which of the following concepts and activities help Demand Management in managing the demand for services?
    1 Differentiated offerings
    2 Differentiated service levels
    3 Major Incident Management
    4 Analysing and tracking the activity patterns of a business process.
  a 4 only
  b 1 and 2 only
  c 1, 2 and 4 only
  d All of the above.

4.6.2 Answers

1 c – Risk analysis involves the identification and assessment of the level of the risks calculated from the assessed values of assets (4) and the assessed levels of threats to (1), and vulnerabilities of (2), those assets, whereas countermeasures (3) are put in place based on the identified risks.

2 c – Option (2) 'practice' is not by itself a determinant for value proposition.

3 d – All of the activities are part of the Service Strategy management process.

4 a – 'Service devaluation' is not an activity in the Financial Management process, whereas 'Service valuation' is.

5 c – Major Incident Management is not a method drawn on by Demand Management.

Service Design

5

5 Service Design

Guidance for the design and development of services, Service Management processes and design capabilities for Service Management.

Design principles and methods for converting strategic objectives into portfolios of services and service assets.

5.1 GOALS AND OBJECTIVES

The main goal is the design of a new or changed service for introduction into the live environment.

The objectives of Service Design are:

- to design services to satisfy business objectives
- to design processes for the design, transition, operation and improvement of IT services
- to identify and manage risks
- to design secure and resilient IT infrastructures, environments, applications and data/information resources and capability
- to design measurement methods and metrics for assessing the effectiveness and efficiency of Service Design
- to produce and maintain IT plans, processes, policies, standards, architectures, frameworks and documents for the design of quality IT solutions
- to develop the skills and capability within IT.

5.2 SCOPE

There are five individual aspects in the scope of Service Design:

1 the design of new or changed *services*
2 the design of the *Service Portfolio*, including the Service Catalogue

3 the design of the *technology architecture and management systems*
4 the design of the *processes*, roles, responsibilities and skills required
5 the design of *measurement methods and metrics*.

Service Design starts with a set of business requirements and ends with the development of a service solution designed to meet the documented needs of the business.

This developed solution design, together with its Service Design Package, is then passed to Service Transition to evaluate, build, test and deploy the new or changed service. On completion of these transition activities, control is transferred to the Service Operation stage of the Service Lifecycle.

5.3 BUSINESS VALUE

With good Service Design it will be possible to deliver quality and cost-effective services, and ensure that the business requirements are being met.

The following benefits are examples of results of good Service Design practice:

- **Reduced total cost of ownership** – cost of ownership can be minimized if all aspects of services, processes and technology are designed properly and implemented against the design.
- **Improved quality and consistency of service** – both service and operational quality will be enhanced and services will be designed within the corporate strategy, architectures and constraints.
- **More effective Service Management and IT processes** – processes will be designed with optimal quality and cost effectiveness.

- **Improved service alignment** – involvement from the conception of the service ensuring that new or changed services match business needs, with services designed to meet SLRs.

5.4 KEY PRINCIPLES

5.4.1 People, processes, products and partners

Good Service Design is dependent on effective and efficient use of the four Ps (Figure 5.1): people, processes, products and partners.

Figre 5.1 The four Ps

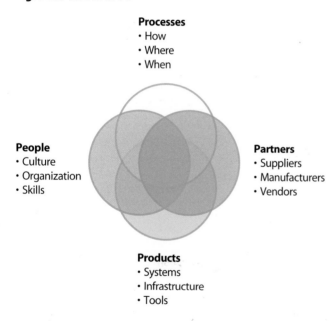

Processes
- How
- Where
- When

People
- Culture
- Organization
- Skills

Partners
- Suppliers
- Manufacturers
- Vendors

Products
- Systems
- Infrastructure
- Tools

Each of these four types of resources has to be prepared, planned and coordinated to achieve an optimal design of services.

5.4.2 The five major aspects of design

An overall, integrated approach should be adopted to the design activities, covering the following five major aspects of design:

1. The design of the *service solutions*, including all of the functional requirements, resources and capabilities needed and agreed.
2. The design of Service Management *systems and tools*, especially the *Service Portfolio* for the management of services through their lifecycle.
3. The design of the *technology architectures* and *management architectures* and tools required to provide the services.
4. The design of the *processes* needed to design, transition, operate and improve the services.
5. The design of the *measurement systems*, methods and metrics for the services, the architectures and their constituent components and the processes.

5.4.2.1 Service solution

A Service Design Package should be produced during the design stage for each new service, for a major change to a service or for the removal of a service.

> **Definition**
> A Service Design Package is a document defining all aspects of an IT service and its requirements through each stage of its lifecycle.

The Service Design Package must contain everything necessary for the subsequent testing, introduction and operation of the solution or service.

This package is then passed from Service Design to Service Transition and details all aspects of the service and its requirements through all of the subsequent stages of its lifecycle.

Figure 5.2 shows the lifecycle of a service from the initial or changed business requirement through the design, transition and operation stages of the lifecycle.

Figure 5.2 Aligning new services to business requirements

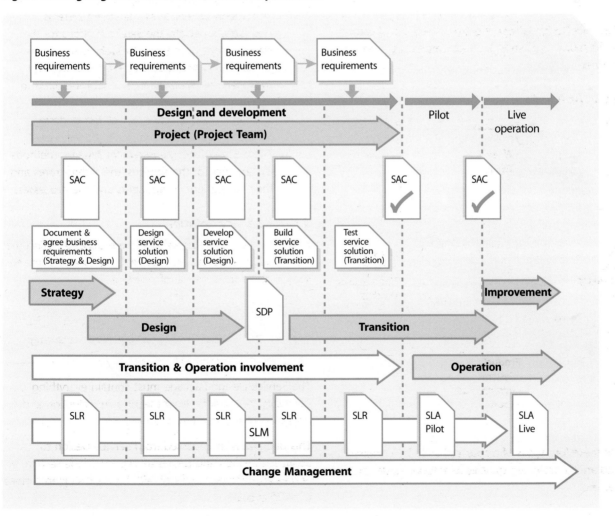

5.4.2.2 Service Portfolio

Each organization should carefully design its Service Portfolio, the content and the access allowed to the content. The content may include:

- Service name
- Service description
- Service status
- Service classification and criticality
- Applications used
- Data and/or data schema used
- Business processes supported
- Business owners
- Business users
- IT owners
- Service warranty level, SLA and SLR references
- Supporting services
- Supporting resources
- Dependent services
- Supporting OLAs, contracts and agreements
- Service costs
- Service charges (if applicable)
- Service revenue (if applicable)
- Service Metrics.

The Service Portfolio represents all the resources presently engaged or being released in various phases of the Service Lifecycle.

The Service Portfolio is used to manage the entire lifecycle of all services, and includes three categories:

1. Service Pipeline (proposed or in development)
2. Service Catalogue (live or available for deployment)
3. Retired services.

Figure 5.3 The Service Portfolio and its contents

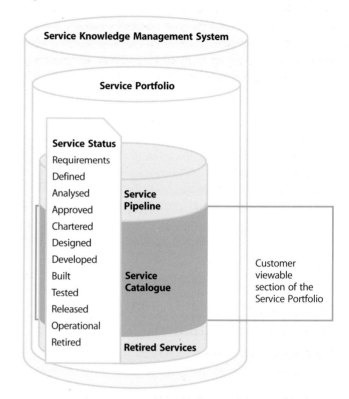

Customers and users would only be allowed access to those services within the Service Portfolio that were of a status between 'Chartered' and 'Operational', as illustrated by the box in Figure 5.3; this is those services contained within the Service Catalogue. The Service Catalogue is the only part of the Portfolio that recovers costs or earns profits.

5.4.2.3 Architecture

The architectural design activities within an IT organization are concerned with providing the overall strategic 'blueprints' for the development and deployment of an IT infrastructure – a set of applications and data which satisfy the current and future needs of the business.

> **Definition**
>
> In this context, Architecture is defined as the structure of a system or an IT service, including the relationships of components to each other and to the environment they are in. Architecture also includes the standards and guidelines which guide the design and evolution of the system.
>
> System in this definition is used in the most general, not necessarily IT, sense as a collection of components organized to accomplish a specific function or set of functions.

The Enterprise Architecture should be an integrated element of the Business Architecture (Figure 5.4).

The Enterprise Architecture should include the following major areas:

- **Service Architecture** – which translates applications, infrastructure, organization and support activities into sets of services
- **Applications Architecture** – which provides a blueprint for the development and deployment of individual applications, maps business and functional requirements onto applications and shows the inter-relationships between applications
- **Data/Information Architecture** – which describes the logical and physical data assets of the enterprise and the data management resources

- **IT Infrastructure Architecture** – which describes the structure, functionality and geographical distribution of the hardware, software, and communications components which underpin and support the overall architecture, together with the technical standards applying to them
- **'Environmental Architecture'** – which describes the all aspects, types and levels of environment controls and their management.

5.4.2.4 Processes

Each organization should adopt a formalized approach to the design and implementation of Service Management processes.

The objective should not be to design 'perfect processes', but to design practical and appropriate processes with 'in-built' improvement mechanisms, so that the effectiveness and efficiency of the processes are improved in the most suitable manner for an organization.

Documentation standards, processes and templates should be used to ensure that the processes are easily adopted throughout the organization.

5.4.2.5 Measurement and metrics

In order to manage and control the design processes they have to be monitored and measured.

There are four types of metrics to measure the capability and performance of processes:

- **Progress:** Milestones and deliverables in the capability of the process.
- **Compliance:** Compliance of the process with governance requirements, regulatory requirements and compliance of people with the use of the process.

Figure 5.4 Architectural relationships

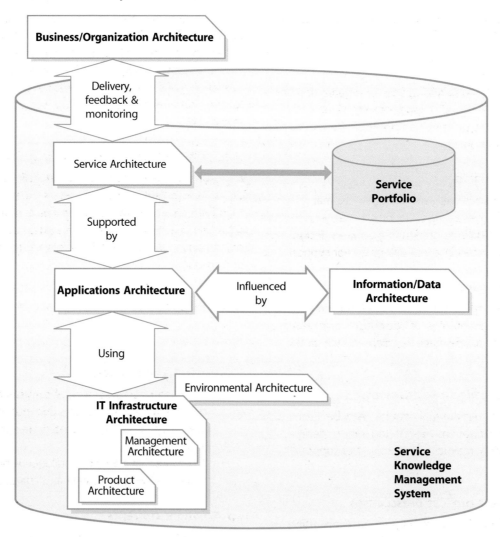

- **Effectiveness:** The accuracy and correctness of the process and its ability to deliver the 'right result'.
- **Efficiency:** The productivity of the process, its speed, throughput and resource utilization.

5.4.3 Sourcing strategies

There are many different delivery options that can be used within Service Design.

5.4.3.1 Insourcing

This approach relies on utilizing internal organizational resources in the design, development, transition, maintenance, operation and/or support of a service or data centre operation.

5.4.3.2 Outsourcing

This approach utilizes the resources of an external organization or organizations in a formal arrangement to provide a well-defined portion of a service's design, development, maintenance, operations and/or support.

5.4.3.3 Co-sourcing

Often the approach is a combination of insourcing and outsourcing, using a number of outsourcing organizations working together to co-source key elements within the lifecycle.

5.4.3.4 Partnership or multisourcing

This approach involves formal arrangements between two or more organizations to work together to design, develop, transition, maintain, operate and/or support IT service(s).

5.4.3.5 Business process outsourcing

This involves relocating entire business functions using formal arrangements between organizations where one organization provides and manages the other organization's entire business process(es) or functions(s) in a low-cost location. Common examples are accounting, payroll and call centre operations.

5.4.3.6 Application service provision

This involves formal arrangements with an Application Service Provider (ASP) organization that will provide shared computer-based services to customer organizations over a network. Through ASPs the complexities and costs of such shared software can be reduced and provided to organizations which could otherwise not justify the investment.

5.4.3.7 Knowledge process outsourcing

Knowledge process outsourcing organizations provide domain-based processes and business expertise rather than just process expertise. This approach requires advanced analytical and specialized skills from the outsourcing organization. It is the newest form of outsourcing.

5.5 PROCESSES

5.5.1 Service Catalogue Management

5.5.1.1 Goals and objectives

- To provide a single source of consistent information on all of the agreed services and ensure that it is widely available to those that are approved to access it.
- To ensure that a Service Catalogue is produced and maintained and is accurate and current.

5.5.1.2 Basic concepts

Definition
The Service Catalogue is a database or structured document with information about all live IT services, including those available for deployment.

The Service Catalogue has two aspects (Figure 5.5):

1 The *Business Service Catalogue* containing details of all of the IT services delivered to the customer, together with relationships to the business units and processes that rely on the IT services. This is the customer view.

2 The *Technical Service Catalogue* containing details of all of the IT services delivered to the customer, together with relationships to the supporting or shared services and Configuration Items (CIs) necessary to support the provision of the service to the business. This should underpin the Business Service Catalogue and not form part of the customer view.

5.5.1.3 Roles

The Service Catalogue Manager has responsibility for producing and maintaining the Service Catalogue. This includes responsibilities such as:

- ensuring that all operational services are recorded within the Service Catalogue
- ensuring that all of the information within the Service Catalogue is accurate and up to date
- ensuring that all of the information within the Service Catalogue is consistent with the information within the Service Portfolio
- ensuring that the information within the Service Catalogue is adequately protected and backed up.

5.5.2 Service Level Management

5.5.2.1 Goals and objectives

- To ensure that an agreed level of IT service is provided for all current IT services and that future services are delivered to agreed achievable targets.
- To define, document, agree, monitor, measure, report and review the level of IT services provided.
- To provide and improve the relationship and communication with the business and customers.

Figure 5.5 The Business Service Catalogue and the Technical Service Catalogue

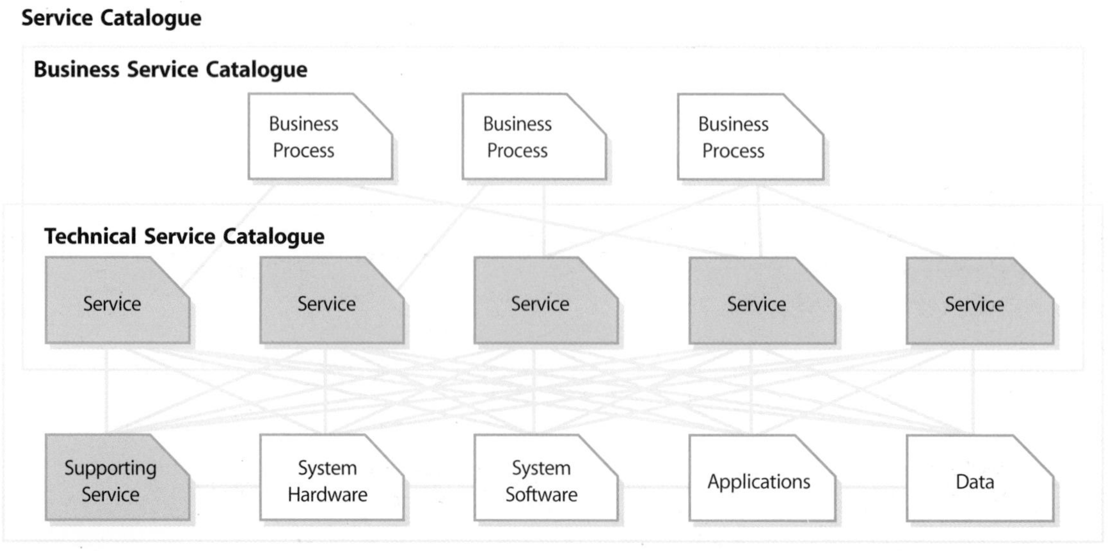

- To ensure that proactive measures to improve the levels of service delivered are implemented wherever it is cost-justifiable to do so.

5.5.2.2 Basic concepts

Definition

A Service Level Agreement (SLA) is an agreement between an IT Service Provider and the IT customer(s). The SLA describes the IT service, service level targets and the responsibilities of the IT Service Provider and the customer. A single SLA may cover multiple IT services or multiple customers.

Definition

A Service Provider is an organization supplying services to one or more internal customers or external customers.

It is necessary to distinguish between different types of Service Provider. There are three archetypes of business model Service Provider:

- Type I – Internal Service Provider
- Type II – Shared Services Unit
- Type III – External Service Provider.

The SLAs are underpinned by OLAs and Underpinning Contracts (Figure 5.6).

Figure 5.6 Service Level Agreements (SLAs), Operational Level Agreements (OLAs) and Underpinning Contracts

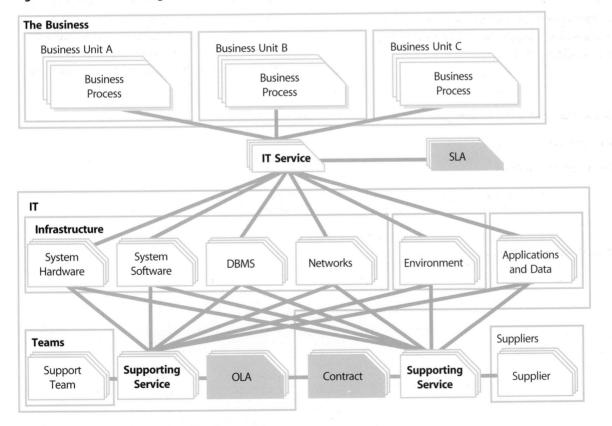

Figure 5.7 The Service Level Management process

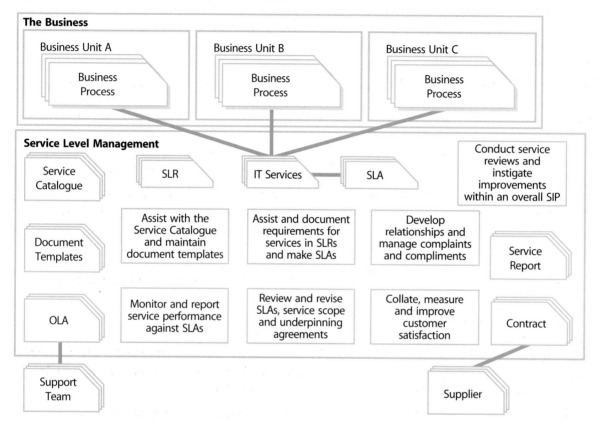

Definition

An Operational Level Agreement (OLA) is an underpinning agreement between an IT Service Provider and another part of the same organization that assists with the provision of services. The OLA defines the goods or services to be provided and the responsibilities of both parties.

For example, there could be an OLA between:

- the IT Service Provider and a procurement department to obtain hardware in agreed times
- the Service Desk and a Support Group to provide Incident resolution in agreed times.

Definition

An Underpinning Contract is a legally binding agreement between an IT Service Provider and a third party, called the supplier. The Underpinning Contract defines targets and responsibilities that are required to meet agreed Service Level Targets in an SLA.

Definition

A supplier is a third party responsible for supplying goods or services that are required to deliver IT services.

Examples of suppliers include commodity hardware and software vendors, network and telecom providers, and outsourcing organizations.

5.5.2.3 Process activities

Service Level Management includes the processes of planning, coordinating, drafting, agreeing, monitoring and reporting of SLAs, and the ongoing review of service achievements to ensure that the required and cost-justifiable service quality is maintained and gradually improved.

The key activities within the Service Level Management process (Figure 5.7) should include:

- designing SLA frameworks, including making available and maintaining up-to-date Service Level Management document templates and standards
- determining, negotiating, documenting and agreeing requirements for new of changed services in SLRs, and managing and reviewing them through the Service Lifecycle into SLAs for operational services
- monitoring and measuring service performance achievements against targets within SLAs
- collating, measuring and improving customer satisfaction
- producing service reports
- conducting service reviews and instigating improvements within an overall Service Improvement Programme
- reviewing and revising SLAs, service scope, Operation Level Agreements, contracts and any other underpinning agreements
- developing and documenting contacts and relationships with the business, customers and stakeholders and managing complaints and compliments

- providing the appropriate management information to aid performance management and demonstrate service achievement.

5.5.2.4 Key metrics

KPIs and metrics can be used to judge the efficiency and effectiveness of the Service Level Management activities and the progress of the Service Improvement Programme. These metrics should be developed from the service, customer and business perspective and should cover both subjective and objective measurements such as:

- improvements in customer satisfaction
- the number or percentage of service targets being met
- the number and severity of service breaches
- the number of services with up-to-date SLAs
- the number of services with timely reports and active service reviews.

5.5.2.5 Roles

The Service Level Manager has responsibility for ensuring that the aims of Service Level Management are met. This includes responsibilities such as:

- ensuring that the service requirements are identified, understood and documented in SLA and SLR documents
- negotiating and agreeing levels of service to be delivered with the customer
- negotiating and agreeing OLAs and other underpinning contracts and agreements
- assisting with the production and maintenance of an accurate Service Portfolio and Service Catalogue
- ensuring that service reports are produced for each customer service and that breaches of SLA targets are managed to prevent their recurrence
- ensuring that improvement initiatives identified in service reviews are acted on and progress reports are provided to customers

- developing relationships and communication with stakeholders, customers and key users, and measurement, recording, analysis and improvement of customer satisfaction.

5.5.2.6 Challenges

Typical challenges faced by Service Level Management include:

- identifying suitable customer representatives with whom to negotiate
- differences in objectives and perceptions of staff at different levels within the customer community
- no past monitored data to confirm that initial targets are achievable
- Service Desk staff commitment to the Service Level Management process, as they are the first contact point for customer enquiries.

5.5.3 Supplier Management

5.5.3.1 Goals and objectives

- To manage suppliers and the services they supply, to provide seamless quality of IT service to the business, ensuring value for money is obtained.
- To ensure that underpinning contracts and agreements with suppliers are aligned to business needs and managed through their lifecycle.
- To manage relationships with suppliers.
- To maintain a supplier policy and a supporting Supplier and Contract Database.

5.5.3.2 Basic concepts

All Supplier Management process activity should be driven by a supplier strategy and policy from Service Strategy (Figure 5.8). In order to achieve consistency and effectiveness in the implementation of the policy, a Supplier and Contracts Database should be established, together with clearly defined roles and responsibilities.

Figure 5.8 Supplier Management process

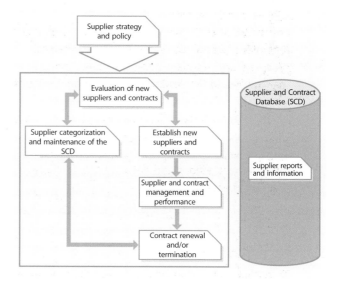

Ideally the Supplier and Contract Database should form an integrated element of a comprehensive Configuration Management System (CMS) and Service Knowledge Management System, recording all supplier and contract details, together with details of the types of services or products provided by each supplier, and all other information and relationships with other associated CIs.

The services provided by suppliers will also form a key part of the Service Portfolio and the Service Catalogue. The relationship between the supporting services and the IT and business services they support are key to providing quality IT services.

5.5.3.3 Roles

The Supplier Manager has responsibility for ensuring that the aims of Supplier Management are met. This includes tasks such as:

- providing assistance in the development and review of Service Level, contracts, agreements or any other documents for third party suppliers

- ensuring that value for money is obtained from IT suppliers and contracts
- ensuring that all IT supplier processes are consistent and interface to all corporate supplier strategies, processes and standard terms and conditions
- maintaining and reviewing a Supplier and Contracts Database
- performing contract or SLA reviews at least annually
- monitoring, reporting and regularly reviewing supplier performance against targets, identifying improvement actions and ensuring these actions are implemented.

5.5.4 Capacity Management

5.5.4.1 Goals and objectives

- To ensure that cost-justifiable IT capacity in all areas of IT always exists and is matched to the current and future agreed needs of the business, in a timely manner.
- To produce and maintain an appropriate and up-to-date Capacity Plan, which reflects the current and future needs of the business.
- To ensure that service performance achievements meet or exceed all of their agreed performance targets.
- To assist with the diagnosis and resolution of capacity-related Incidents and Problems and assessment of the impact of all changes on capacity and resources.

5.5.4.2 Basic concepts

Capacity Management is essentially a balancing act:

- balancing *costs* against *resources* needed
- balancing *supply* against *demand*.

The overall Capacity Management process (Figure 5.9) is continually trying to cost-effectively match IT resources and capacity to the ever-changing needs and requirements of the business. This requires tuning and optimization of current resources and effective estimation and planning of future resources.

The Capacity Management process consists of three sub-processes:

1 The *Business Capacity Management* sub-process translates business needs and plans into requirements for service and IT infrastructure.

2 The *Service Capacity Management* sub-process focuses on the management, control and prediction of the end-to-end performance and capacity of the operational IT services usage and workloads.

3 The *Component Capacity Management* sub-process focuses on the management, control and prediction of the performance, utilization and capacity of individual IT technology components.

Figure 5.9 The Capacity Management process

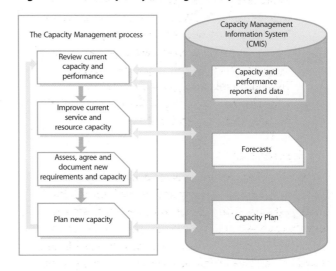

5.5.4.3 Roles

The Capacity Manager has responsibility for ensuring that the aims of Capacity Management are met. This includes such tasks as:

- overall responsibility for ensuring that there is adequate IT capacity to meet required levels of service
- identifying current capacity requirements and forecasting future capacity requirements based on business plans, usage trends, sizing of new services etc.
- production, regular review and revision of the Capacity Plan
- performing sizing on all proposed new services and systems
- analysis of usage and performance data, and reporting on performance against SLA targets
- identifying and initiating any tuning to be carried out to optimize and improve capacity or performance
- assisting with the diagnosis and resolution of capacity and performance-related Incidents and Problems, and assessment of the impact of all changes on capacity and performance.

5.5.5 Availability Management

5.5.5.1 Goals and objectives

- To ensure that the level of service availability delivered in all services is matched to or exceeds the current and future agreed needs of the business, in a cost-effective manner.
- To produce and maintain an appropriate and up-to-date Availability Plan, which reflects the needs of the business.

- To assist with the diagnosis and resolution of availability-related Incidents and Problems, and assessment of the impact of all changes on availability.
- To ensure that proactive measures to improve the availability of services are implemented wherever it is cost-justifiable to do so.

5.5.5.2 Basic concepts

Definition
Availability is the ability of a service, component or CI to perform its agreed function when required.

Availability is usually calculated as a percentage. This calculation is often based on agreed service time and downtime. It is best practice to calculate availability using measurements of the business output of the IT service.

A good technique to help with the technical analysis of Incidents affecting the availability of IT services and components is to take an *Incident 'lifecycle' view*.

Every Incident passes through several major stages which can be timed and measured. The time elapsed in these stages may vary considerably. Figure 5.10 illustrates the expanded Incident 'lifecycle'.

Availability Management should perform both reactive and proactive activities (Figure 5.11).

The reactive activities of Availability Management consist of monitoring, measuring, analysing, reporting and reviewing all aspects of service and component availability.

The *proactive activities* consist of producing recommendations, plans and documents on design guidelines and criteria for new and changed services, and the continual improvement of service and reduction of risk in existing services wherever it can be cost-justified. These are key aspects to be considered within Service Design activities.

5.5.5.3 Roles

The Availability Manager has responsibility for ensuring that the aims of Availability Management are met. This includes responsibilities such as:

■ ensuring that all existing services deliver the levels of availability agreed with the business in SLAs

■ ensuring that all new services are designed to deliver the levels of availability required by the business and validation of the design to meet the agreed levels of availability

■ assisting with the diagnosis and resolution of availability-related Incidents and Problems and assessment of the impact of all changes on availability

■ monitoring of actual IT availability achieved against SLA targets and reporting of IT availability to ensure that agreed levels of availability are measured and monitored on an ongoing basis

■ proactively improving service availability wherever possible and optimizing the availability of the IT infrastructure to deliver cost-effective improvements that deliver tangible benefits to the business.

Figure 5.10 The expanded Incident lifecycle

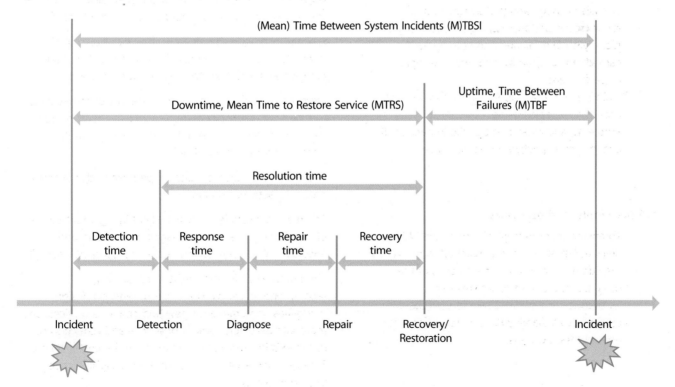

Figure 5.11 The Availability Management process

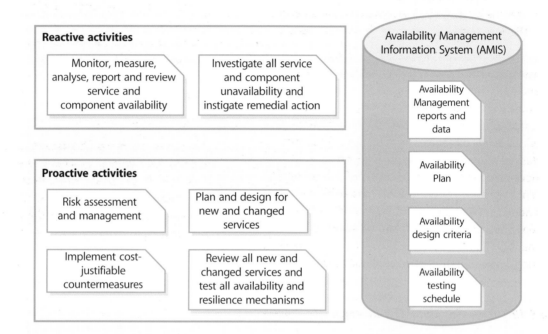

5.5.6 Service Continuity Management

5.5.6.1 Goals and objectives

- To support the overall Business Continuity Management process by ensuring that the required service facilities can be resumed within required, and agreed, business timescales.
- To maintain a set of IT Service Continuity and IT recovery plans that support the overall Business Continuity Plans of an organization.
- To ensure that all continuity plans are maintained in line with changing business impacts, requirements and risks through regular Business Impact Analysis exercises and risk assessments.

- To ensure that appropriate continuity and recovery mechanisms are put in place to meet or exceed the agreed business continuity targets.

5.5.6.2 Basic concepts

Figure 5.12 shows the role played within the Service Continuity Management process of Business Continuity Management.

Service Continuity Management is a cyclical process through the lifecycle to ensure that once service continuity and recovery plans have been developed, they are kept aligned with Business Continuity Plans and business priorities.

5.5.6.3 Roles

The Service Continuity Manager has responsibility for ensuring that the aims of Service Continuity Management are met. This includes such tasks and responsibilities as:

- performing Business Impact Analysis, risk assessment and risk management for all existing and all new services
- implementing and maintaining the Service Continuity Management process in accordance with the overall requirements of the organization's Business Continuity Management process
- developing and ensuring that all Service Continuity Management strategies, plans, risks and activities underpin and align with all Business Continuity Management strategies, plans, risks and activities
- maintaining a comprehensive IT testing schedule, including the testing of all continuity plans

- undertaking regular reviews, at least annually, of the Continuity Plans with the business areas to ensure that they accurately reflect the business needs
- assessing changes for their impact on service continuity and Continuity Plans.

5.5.7 Information Security Management

5.5.7.1 Goals and objectives

- To align IT security with business security and ensure that information security is effectively managed in all Service Management activities.
- To ensure that that the information security risks are appropriately managed and enterprise information resources are used responsibly.

Figure 5.12 The Service Continuity Management process

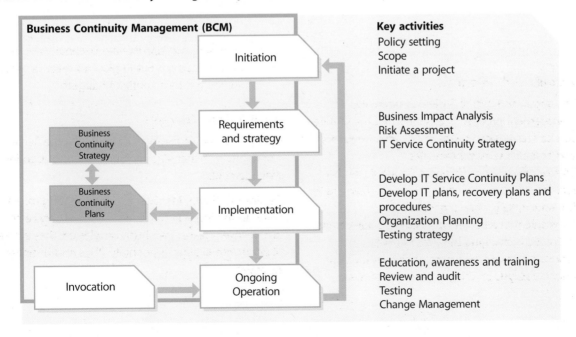

- To protect the interests of those relying on information, and the systems and communications that deliver the information, from harm resulting from failures of availability, confidentiality and integrity.

5.5.7.2 Basic concepts

The Information Security Management process and framework (Figure 5.13) will generally consist of:

- an *Information Security Policy* and specific security policies that address each aspect of strategy, controls and regulation. The policies should be widely available to all customers and users
- an *Information Security Management System* (ISMS), containing the standards, management procedures and guidelines supporting the information security policies
- a comprehensive *Security Strategy* closely linked to the business objectives, strategies and plans
- an effective *security organization*
- a set of *security controls* to support the Information Security Policy
- the *management of security risks*
- *monitoring of processes* to ensure compliance and effectiveness

- *a communications, training and awareness strategy* and a plan for security.

The ISMS in Figure 5.13 shows an approach which is widely used and is based on the advice and guidance described in ISO 27001.

5.5.7.3 Roles

The Security Manager has responsibility for ensuring that the aims of Information Security Management are met. This includes such tasks and responsibilities as:

- developing, maintaining, communicating and publicizing the Information Security Policy and a supporting set of specific policies
- ensuring that the Information Security Policy is enforced and adhered to
- identifying and classifying IT and information assets and the level of control and protection required
- performing security risk analysis and risk management
- designing and maintaining security controls, plans and procedures
- monitoring security breaches and managing security Incidents.

Figure 5.13 Framework for managing IT security

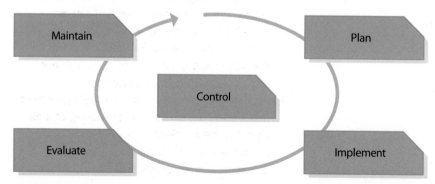

5.6 SAMPLE QUESTIONS AND ANSWERS

5.6.1 Questions

1 Which of the following statements is NOT an objective of Service Design?
   a To design services to satisfy business objectives
   b To identify and manage risks
   c To plan and manage the resources to successfully establish a new or changed service into production with the predicted cost, quality and time estimates
   d To design efficient and effective processes for the design, transition, operation and improvement of high-quality IT services.

2 Which of the following statements are CORRECT?
   a A Service Provider is an organization supplying services to one or more external customers.
   b A Service Provider is an organization supplying services to one or more internal customers or external customers.
   c A Service Provider is a third party responsible for supplying goods or underpinning services that are required to deliver IT services.
   d A Service Provider is a role that has responsibility for ensuring that all new services are designed to deliver the levels of availability required by the business and validation of the final design to meet the minimum levels of availability as agreed by the business for IT services.

3 Which of the following are the five major aspects of Service Design?
   1 Service Portfolio design
   2 Technology and architectural design
   3 Design of services
   4 Strategy design
   5 Process design
   6 Measurement design
   a 1, 2, 3, 4 and 5
   b 1, 2, 4, 5 and 6

   c 1, 2, 3, 5 and 6
   d 2, 3, 4, 5 and 6

4 Which of the following is NOT a sourcing approach?
   a Insourcing
   b Co-sourcing
   c Rightsourcing
   d Application Service Provision.

5 Which of the following activities is an activity in the Service Level Management process?
   a Collate, measure and improve customer satisfaction
   b Status reporting
   c Deploy Service Component
   d Resolution and Recovery.

6 Which of the following metrics is BEST used to judge the efficiency and effectiveness of the Service Level Management process?
   a Number and percentage of major Incidents
   b The number and severity of service breaches
   c Reduction in the number of disruptions to services caused by inaccurate impact assessment
   d Reduction in the costs of handling printer Incidents.

7 Consider the following roles and responsibilities:
   A Availability Manager
   B Service Catalogue Manager
   C Supplier Manager
   D Capacity Manager.
   1 Analysis of usage and performance data, and reporting on performance against targets contained in Service Level Agreements.
   2 Ensuring that all of the information within the Service Catalogue is consistent with the information within the Service Portfolio.
   3 Performing contract or Service Level Agreement reviews at least annually and ensuring that all contracts are consistent with organizational requirements and standard terms and conditions wherever possible.

4 Ensuring that all existing services deliver the levels of availability agreed with the business in Service Level Agreements.

■ Which of the following pairings between the roles and responsibilities is CORRECT?
a   A–1, B–3, C–2 and D–4
b   A–1, B–2, C–3 and D–4
c   A–2, B–3, C–4 and D–1
d   A–4, B–2, C–3 and D–1

8 Which of the following is NOT a sub-process of the Capacity Management process?
a   Component Capacity Management
b   Configuration Capacity Management
c   Business Capacity Management
d   Service Capacity Management.

5.6.2 Answers

1 c – This is one of the objectives of Service Transition.

2 b – Option (a) is incorrect because a Service Provider can provide services internally (called a type I or II Service Provider). Option (c) is the definition of a Supplier, and option (d) is a responsibility for the Availability Manager.

3 c – Strategy design is part of the Service Strategy stage of the lifecycle.

4 c – Rightsourcing is a popular way of saying that you need to make the right mix of the sourcing approaches.

5 a – Option (b) is an activity from the Service Asset and Configuration Management process, option (c) is an activity from the Release and Deployment Management process and option (d) is an activity form the Incident Management process.

6 b – Option (a) is an example of an Incident Management metric, option (c) is an example of a metric to measure the efficiency and effectiveness of the Change Management process, and option (d) is an example of a Continual Service Improvement metric.

7 d

8 b – There is nothing in ITIL called Configuration Capacity Management.

Service Transition

6

6 Service Transition

Guidance for the development and improvement of capabilities for transitioning new and changed services into operations.

Guidance on managing the complexity related to changes to services and service management processes; preventing undesired consequences while allowing for innovation.

6.1 GOALS AND OBJECTIVES

The main goals of Service Transition are:

- to enable the business change project or customer to integrate a release into their business processes and services
- to reduce Known Errors and minimize the risks from transitioning the new or changed services into production
- to ensure that the service can be used in accordance with the requirements and constraints specified within the service requirements.

The objectives of Service Transition are:

- to plan and manage the resources to successfully establish a new or changed service into production within the predicted cost, quality and time estimates
- to ensure there is minimal unpredicted impact on the production services, operations and support organization
- to increase the customer, user and service management staff satisfaction with the Service Transition practices

- to increase proper use of the services and underlying applications and technology
- to provide clear and comprehensive plans that enable the customer and business change projects to align their activities with the Service Transition plans.

6.2 SCOPE

The scope of Service Transition (Figure 6.1) includes the management and coordination of the processes, systems and functions to package, build, test and deploy a release into production and establish the service specified in the customer and stakeholder requirements.

The following activities are excluded from the scope of Service Transition best practices:

- minor modifications to the production services and environment, e.g. replacement of a failed PC or registration of a new user
- ongoing Continual Service Improvements that do not significantly impact on the services or Service Provider's capability to deliver the services.

Service Transition activities are shown in the white boxes in Figure 6.1. The dark boxes represent activities in the other stages of the Service Lifecycle.

The following lifecycle processes in the Service Transition stage support all lifecycle stages:

- Change Management
- Service Asset and Configuration Management
- Knowledge Management.

Figure 6.1 The scope of Service Transition

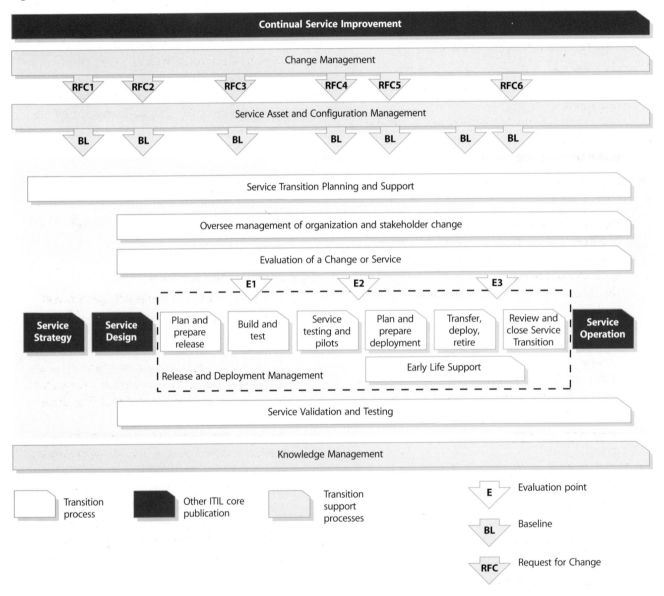

6.3 BUSINESS VALUE

Effective Service Transition can significantly improve a Service Provider's ability to handle high volumes of change and releases. It enables the Service Provider to:

- align the new or changed service with the customer's business requirements and business operations
- ensure that customers and users can use the new or changed service in a way that maximizes value to the business operations.

Specifically, Service Transition adds value to the business by improving:

- the ability to adapt quickly to new requirements and market developments ('competitive edge')
- transition management of mergers, de-mergers, acquisitions, transfer of services
- the success rate of changes and releases for the business
- confidence in the degree of compliance with business and governance requirements during change.
- understanding the level of risk during and after change, e.g. service outage, disruption, re-work.

6.4 KEY PRINCIPLES

The Service V-model builds in service validation and testing early in the Service Lifecycle.

Figure 6.2 provides an example of the V-model used to represent the different levels of Configuration Items to be built, managed, validated and tested to deliver a Service Capability.

The left-hand side represents the specification of the service requirements down to the detailed Service Design.

The right-hand side focuses on the validation activities that are performed against the specifications defined on the left-hand side.

At each stage on the left hand side, there is direct involvement by the equivalent party on the right-hand side. Service validation and acceptance test planning should start with the definition of the service requirements. For example, customers who sign off the agreed service requirements will also sign off the service acceptance criteria and test plan.

6.5 PROCESSES

6.5.1 Service Asset and Configuration Management

6.5.1.1 Goals and objectives

- To support efficient and effective business and Service Management processes by providing accurate information about assets and Configuration Items.
- To provide a logical model of the services, assets and different components (physical, logical etc.) and their relationships needed to deliver these services.
- To define and control the components of services and infrastructure and maintain accurate configuration records.
- To enable an organization to comply with corporate governance requirements, control its asset base, optimize its costs, manage change and releases effectively, and resolve Incidents and problems faster.

Figure 6.2 The Service V-model

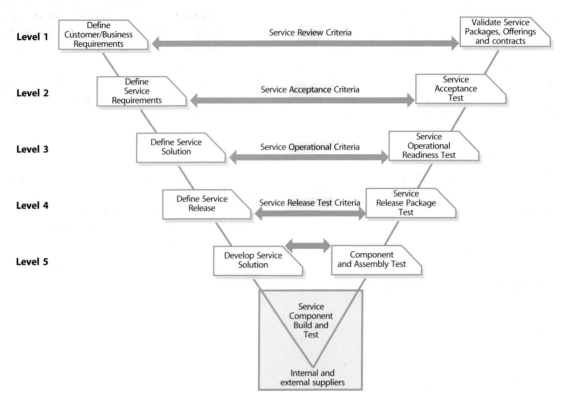

6.5.1.2 Basic concepts

Definition

A Configuration Item (CI) is any component that needs to be managed in order to deliver an IT service.

Information about each CI is recorded in a configuration record within the CMS and is maintained throughout its lifecycle by Configuration Management. CIs are under the control of Change Management.

CIs may vary widely in complexity, size and type, ranging from an entire service or system including all hardware, software, documentation and support staff to a single software module or a minor hardware component.

There will be a variety of CIs. The following categories may help to identify them.

- **Service Lifecycle CIs** – such as the Business Case, Service Management plans, Service Lifecycle plans, Service Design Package, Release and Change plans, Test plans
- **Service CIs** – such as Service Capability assets (management, organization, processes, knowledge, people), service resource assets (financial capital, systems, applications, information, data, infrastructure and facilities, financial capital, people), Service Model, Service Package, Release Package, Service Acceptance Criteria

- **Organization CIs** – such as an organization's business strategy or other policies
- **Internal CIs** – comprising those delivered by individual projects, including assets such as hardware and software that are required to deliver and maintain the service and infrastructure
- **External CIs** – such as external customer requirements and agreements, releases from Suppliers or sub-contractors and external services.

Configuration management delivers a logical model of the services, assets and the infrastructure by recording the relationships between CIs as shown in Figure 6.3. This enables other processes to access valuable information such as:

- to assess the impact and cause of Incidents and problems
- to assess the impact of proposed changes

- to plan and design new or changed services
- to plan technology refresh and software upgrades
- to plan release and deployment packages and migrate service assets to different locations and service centres
- to optimize asset utilization and costs, e.g. consolidate data centres, reduce variations, and reuse assets.

> **Definition**
> A Service Knowledge Management System is a set of tools and databases that are used to manage knowledge and information. The SKMS stores, manages, updates, and presents all information that an IT Service Provider needs to manage the full lifecycle of IT services.

Figure 6.3 Example of a logical configuration model

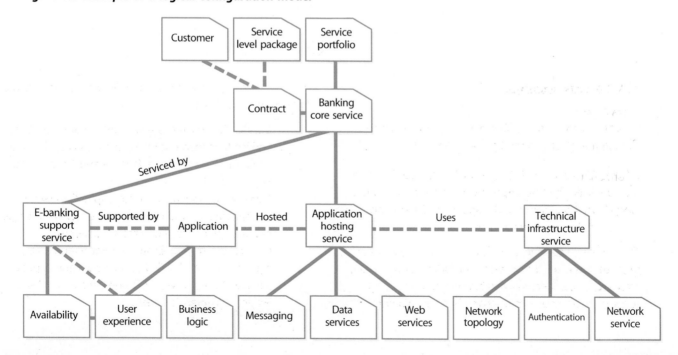

Figure 6.4 Example of a Service Knowledge Management System

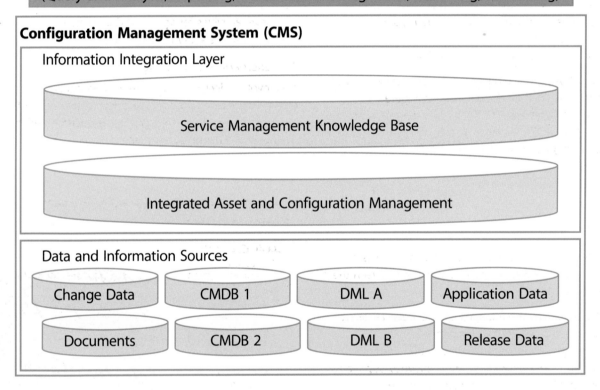

The Service Knowledge Management System includes the CMS and Configuration Management Databases, as well as other tools and databases.

However, clearly the Service Knowledge Management System is a broader concept that covers a much wider base of knowledge, for example:

- the experience of staff
- records of peripheral matters, e.g. user numbers and an organization's performance figures.
- Supplier and partners' requirements, abilities and expectations
- typical and anticipated user skill levels.

Figure 6.4 illustrates the relationship of the three levels, with data being gathered within the Configuration Management Database (CMDB), and feeding through the CMS into the Service Knowledge Management System and supporting the informed decision-making process.

> **Definition**
> A Configuration Management System is a set of tools and databases that are used to manage an IT Service Provider's configuration data.

The CMS will hold details of all of the components of the IT infrastructure as well as the relationships between these components.

The CMS maintains the relationships between all service components and any related Incidents, Problems, Known Errors, Change and Release documentation and may also contain corporate data about employees, suppliers, locations and business units, customers and users.

At the data level, the CMS may take data from several physical CMDBs, which together constitute a federated CMDB. Other data sources will also plug into the CMS such as the Definitive Media Libraries. The CMS will provide access to data in asset inventories wherever possible rather than duplicating data.

The CMS typically contains configuration data and information that is combined into an integrated set of views for different stakeholders through the Service Lifecycle. It therefore needs to be based on appropriate web, reporting and database technologies that provide flexible and powerful visualization and mapping tools, interrogation and reporting facilities.

The CMS is maintained by Configuration Management and is used by all IT Service Management processes.

High-level activities for asset and Configuration Management are shown in Figure 6.5.

Management and planning

This involves deciding what level of Configuration Management is required for the selected services and how this level will be achieved. This is documented in a Configuration Management plan.

Figure 6.5 The Service Asset and Configuration Management process

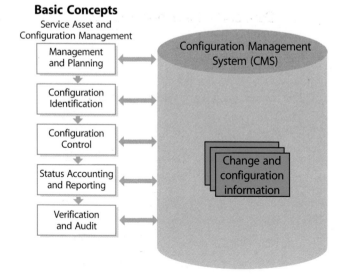

Configuration identification

When planning configuration identification it is important to define:

- how the classes and types of assets and Configuration Items are to be selected, grouped, classified and defined by appropriate characteristics
- the approach to identification, uniquely naming and labelling all the components of interest and the relationships between them
- the roles and responsibilities of the owner or custodian for CI type at each stage of its lifecycle.

Configuration control

Configuration control ensures that there are adequate control mechanisms over CIs while maintaining a record of changes to status, approvals, location and custodianship/ownership.

Status accounting and reporting

Each CI will have one or more discrete states through which it can progress. The significance of each state should be defined in terms of what use can be made of the CI.

Verification and audit

The activities include a series of reviews or audits to ensure that there is conformity between the documented baselines (e.g. agreements, interface control documents) and the actual business environment to which they refer.

6.5.1.3 Roles

Service Asset/Configuration Manager

The Service Configuration Manager's responsibilities include the following:

- implementing the organization's Service Asset and Configuration Management policy and standards
- agreeing the scope of the Asset and Configuration Management processes, function, the items that are to be controlled, and the information that is to be recorded; developing standards, plans and procedures
- managing the Configuration Management plan, principles and processes and their implementation
- agreeing the assets/CIs to be uniquely identified with naming conventions
- planning and managing the Asset and Configuration Management System.

Configuration Analyst

The Configuration Analyst:

- creates Asset and Configuration Management processes and procedures
- uses or provides the Asset and CMS to facilitate impact on assessment for RFCs and faults that are affecting a CI
- performs configuration audits to check that the physical IT inventory is consistent with the Asset and Configuration Management System and initiates any necessary corrective action.

Configuration Administrator/Librarian

The Configuration Administrator is the custodian and guardian of all master copies of software, assets and documentation CIs registered with Asset and Configuration Management.

Configuration Management System/Tools Administrator

The Tools Administrator evaluates proprietary Asset and Configuration Management tools, and recommends, implements and customizes those that best meet the organization's budget, resource, timescales and technical requirements.

6.5.2 Change Management

6.5.2.1 Goals and objectives

- To respond to the customer's changing business requirements while maximizing value and reducing Incidents, disruption and re-work.
- To respond to the business and IT requests for change that will integrate the services with the business needs.
- To ensure that changes are recorded and then evaluated, authorized, prioritized, planned, tested, implemented, documented and reviewed in a controlled manner.

6.5.2.2 Scope

The scope of Change Management covers changes to baselined service assets and CIs across the whole Service Lifecycle.

Each organization should define the changes that lie inside the scope of their service change process. Typically these might include:

- changes with significantly wider impacts than service changes, e.g. departmental organization, policies, business operations. These changes produce RFCs to generate consequential service changes
- changes at an operational level such as repair to printers or other routine service components.

6.5.2.3 Basic concepts

Definition

A Change is the addition, modification or removal of anything that could have an effect on IT services. The scope should include processes, documentation etc.

6.5.2.4 Change types

Changes can be divided into three types:

1 Normal Change

Normal Change (Figure 6.6) typically includes change requests such as:

- RFC to the Service Portfolios
- RFC to a service
- Project change proposal
- User access request
- Operational activity.

2 Standard Change

A Standard Change is a change to a service or infrastructure for which the approach is preauthorized by Change Management that has an accepted and established procedure to provide a specific change requirement.

The crucial elements of a Standard Change are that:

- there is a defined trigger to initiate the RFC
- the tasks are well known, documented and proven
- authority is effectively given in advance
- budgetary approval will typically be preordained or within the control of the Change requester
- usually low risk, and always well-understood risk.

3 Emergency Change

Emergency Change is reserved for changes intended to repair an error in an IT service that is negatively impacting on the business to a high degree. Changes intended to introduce immediately required business improvements are handled as Normal Changes, assessed as having the highest urgency.

Defined authorization levels will exist for an Emergency Change, and the levels of delegated authority must be clearly documented and understood. In an emergency situation it may not be possible to convene a full CAB meeting. Where CAB approval is required, this will be provided by the Emergency CAB.

Figure 6.6 Example process flow for a Normal Change

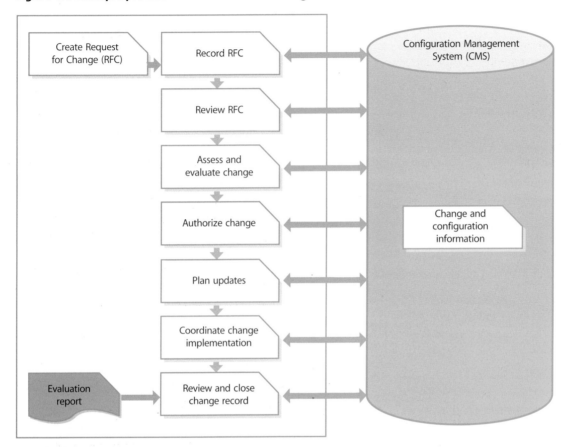

6.5.2.5 The seven Rs of Change Management

The following questions must be answered for all changes. Without this information, the impact assessment cannot be completed, and the balance of risk and benefit to the live service will not be understood:

- Who RAISED the change?
- What is the REASON for the change?
- What is the RETURN required from the change?
- What are the RISKS involved in the change?
- What RESOURCES are required to deliver the change?
- Who is RESPONSIBLE for the build, test and implementation of the change?
- What is the RELATIONSHIP between this change and other changes?

6.5.2.6 Process activities

Overall Change Management activities include:

- Planning and controlling changes
- Change and release scheduling
- Communications
- Change decision making and change authorization

- Ensuring there are remediation plans
- Measurement and control
- Management reporting
- Understanding the impact of change
- Continual improvement.

Typical activities in managing individual changes are:

- to create and record changes
- to review and filter RFCs and the change proposal
- to assess and evaluate the change:
  - establish appropriate level of change authority
  - establish relevant areas of interest (i.e. who should be involved in the CAB)
  - assess and evaluate the business justification, impact, cost, benefits and risk of changes
  - request independent evaluation of a change
- to authorize the change:
  - obtain authorization/rejection
  - communicate the decision to all stakeholders, in particular the initiator of the RFC
- to plan updates
- to coordinate change implementation
- to review and close each change.

6.5.2.7 Key metrics

Some of the KPIs for Change Management are:

- the percentage of changes implemented to services which met the customer's agreed requirements, e.g. quality/cost/time
- reduction in the number of disruptions to services, defects and re-work caused by changes
- reduction in the number of unauthorized changes
- reduction in the backlog of change requests
- reduction in the number and percentage of unplanned changes and emergency fixes
- the change success rate
- the average time to implement based on urgency/ priority/change type
- Incidents attributable to changes.

6.5.2.8 Roles

Change Manager

The main duties of the Change Manager, some of which may be delegated, are to:

- receive, log and allocate a priority, in collaboration with the initiator, to all RFCs
- table all RFCs for a CAB meeting, issue an agenda and circulate all RFCs to CAB members in advance of meetings
- convene Emergency CAB meetings for all urgent RFCs
- chair all CAB and Emergency CAB meetings
- authorize acceptable changes
- liaise with all necessary parties to coordinate change building, testing and implementation, in accordance with schedules
- review all implemented changes to ensure that they have met their objectives. Refer back any that have been backed out or have failed
- close RFCs
- produce regular and accurate management reports.

CAB member

The CAB is a body that exists to support the authorization of changes and to assist Change Management in the assessment and prioritization of changes.

As and when a CAB is convened, the members who are chosen should be individuals capable of ensuring that all changes within the scope of the CAB are adequately assessed from both a business and a technical viewpoint.

6.5.2.9 Challenges

Typical challenges faced by Change Management are:

- unauthorized changes
- lack of knowledge of impacted systems making impact assessment impossible
- resistance to a process perceived as bureaucratic
- lack of an accurate CMS.

6.5.3 Release and Deployment Management

6.5.3.1 *Goals and objectives*

- To deploy releases into production and enable effective use of the service in order to deliver value to the customer.
- To ensure that there are clear and comprehensive release and deployment plans that enable the customer and business change projects to align their activities with these plans.
- To ensure that a release package can be built, installed, tested and deployed efficiently successfully and on schedule.
- To ensure that a new or changed service and its enabling systems, technology and organization are capable of delivering the agreed service requirements, i.e. utilities, warranties and service levels.
- To transfer knowledge customers and users to optimize their use of the service.
- To transfer skills and knowledge to operations and support staff to enable them to effectively and efficiently deliver, support and maintain the service.

6.5.3.2 *Basic concepts*

> **Definition**
> A Release Unit is a collection of components of an IT service that are normally released together according to an organization's release policy.

A Release Unit typically includes sufficient components to perform a useful function. For example one Release Unit could be a desktop PC, including hardware, software, licences, documentation etc. Another Release Unit may be the complete payroll application, including IT operations procedures and user training.

The unit may vary, depending on the types or items of service asset or service component, such as software and hardware. Figure 6.7 is a simplified example showing an IT service made up of systems and service assets, which are in turn made up of service components.

The general aim is to decide the most appropriate Release-Unit level for each service asset or component. An organization may, for example, decide that the Release Unit for business-critical applications is the complete application in order to ensure that testing is comprehensive. The same organization may decide that a more appropriate Release Unit for a website is at the page level.

A Release Package may be a single Release Unit or a structured set of release units.

> **Definition**
> A Definitive Media Library is one or more locations in which the definitive and approved versions of all software CIs are securely stored. The Definitive Media Library may also contain associated CIs such as licences and documentation.

The Definitive Media Library should include definitive copies of purchased software (along with licence documents or information), as well as software developed on site. Master copies of controlled documentation for a system are also stored in the Definitive Media Library in electronic form.

The Definitive Media Library will also include a physical store to hold master copies, e.g. a fireproof safe.

Figure 6.7 Simplified example of release units for an IT service

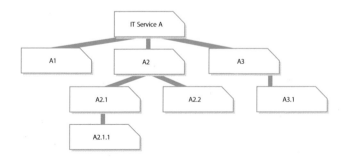

All software in the Definitive Media Library is under the control of Change and Release Management and is recorded in the Configuration Management System (Figure 6.8) strictly controlled by Service Asset and Configuration Management.

Any significant new or changed service or service offering will require the deployment stage to consider the full range of elements comprising that service – infrastructure, hardware, software, applications, documentation, knowledge etc. Effectively this means the deployment will contain sub-deployments for elements comprising the service, as illustrated in Figure 6.9. The combination, relationship and interdependencies of these components will require careful and considered planning. Significant deployments will be complex projects in their own right.

Several options and combinations exist for deploying new releases to multiple locations:

- **Big-bang** – the new or changed service is deployed to all user areas in one operation.
- **Phased approach** – the service is deployed to a part of the user base initially, and then this operation is repeated for subsequent parts of the user base via a scheduled roll-out plan.

Figure 6.8 Relationship between the Definitive Media Library and the Configuration Management Database

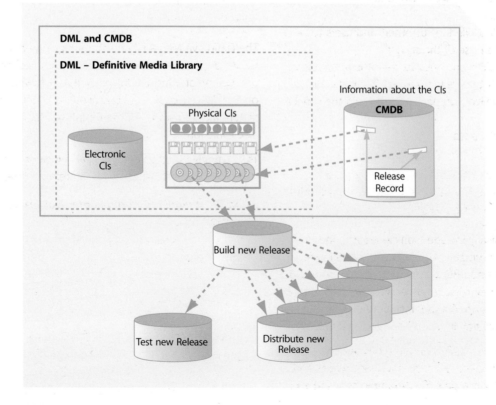

Figure 6.9 The Release and Deployment process: coordinating the deployment of service components

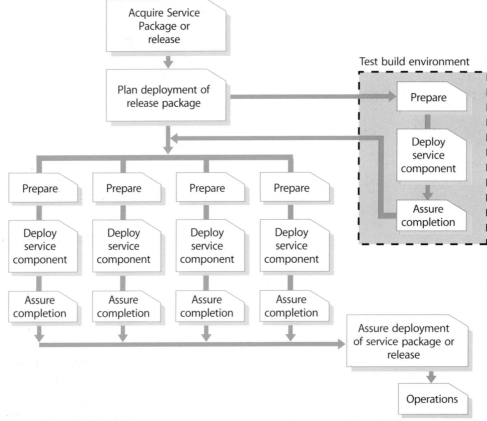

- **A Push approach** – the service component is deployed from the centre and pushed out to the target locations. The new or changed service is delivered into the user's environment at a time not of their choosing.
- **A Pull approach** – the software is made available in a central location but users are free to pull the software down to their own location at a time of their choosing or when a user workstation restarts.
- **Automation** will help to ensure repeatability and consistency.

- If a **manual mechanism** is used it is important to monitor and measure the impact of many repeated manual activities as they are likely to be inefficient and error prone. Too many manual activities will slow down the release team and create resource/capacity issues that affect the service levels.

6.5.3.3 Roles

Release and Deployment Manager

The Release and Deployment Manager is responsible for the planning, design, build, configuration and testing of all software and hardware to create the Release Package for the delivery of, or changes to, the designated service.

The overall responsibilities of the Release and Deployment Manager are:

- coordination of build and test environment team and release teams
- provision of management reports on Release progress
- service Release and Deployment policy and planning
- Release package design, build and configuration
- Release package acceptance, including business sign-off
- service roll-out planning, including method of deployment
- Release Package testing to predefined acceptance criteria
- sign-off of the release Package for implementation
- communication, preparation and training
- storage and traceability/audit ability of controlled software in both centralized and distributed systems
- release, distribution and installation of packaged software.

Release Packaging and Build Manager

The main duties of the Release Packaging and Build Manager are:

- establishing the final Release configuration
- building the final Release delivery
- testing the final delivery prior to independent testing
- establishing and reporting outstanding Known Errors and Workarounds
- providing input to the final implementation sign-off process.

Deployment Manager

The Deployment Manager is responsible for the following activities:

- final physical delivery of the service implementation
- coordinating release documentation and communications, including training and customer service management and technical release notes
- planning the deployment
- providing technical and application guidance and support throughout the release process, including Known Errors and Workarounds
- recording metrics for deployment to ensure they are within agreed SLAs.

6.6   SAMPLE QUESTIONS AND ANSWERS

6.6.1   Questions

1   Service Transition adds value to the business by improving:
   a   the management of the technology that is used to deliver and support services
   b   the success rate of changes and releases for the business
   c   the design of the IT processes
   d   the organizational competency for Continual Service Improvement.

2   Which of the following is NOT a Change type?
   a   Normal Change
   b   Emergency Change
   c   Known Change
   d   Standard Change

3   Which of the following statements about the Service V-model are CORRECT?
   1   Using a model such as the V-model builds in service validation and testing early in the Service Lifecycle.

2 The left-hand side of the V-model represents the specification of the service requirements down to the detailed Service Design.

3 The right-hand side of the V-model focuses on the validation activities that are performed against the specifications defined on the left-hand side.

4 Customers who sign off the agreed service requirements will also sign off the Service Acceptance Criteria and test plan.

a   1 only
b   2 and 3 only
c   1, 2 and 3 only
d   All of the above.

4 Consider the following activities from the Change Management process:

1 Review the Change
2 Assess and evaluate the Change
3 Authorize the Change
4 Coordinate Change implementation
5 Review Request for Change.

Which of the following options describes the CORRECT order of the activities?

a   1, 2, 3, 4, 5
b   1, 3, 4, 2, 5
c   5, 3, 2, 4, 1
d   5, 2, 3, 4, 1

5 Which of the following statements about the Configuration Management System are CORRECT?

1 It will hold details of all of the components of the IT infrastructure as well as the relationships between these components.

2 At the data level, it consists of one and only one physical Configuration Management Database.

3 The Service Knowledge Management System includes the Configuration Management System.

4 It is maintained by Service Asset and Configuration Management.

a   1 only
b   2 and 3 only
c   1, 3 and 4 only
d   All of the above.

6.6.2 Answers

1   b – Option (a) is a benefit of Service Operation, option (c) is a benefit of Service Design and option (d) is a benefit of Continual Service Improvement.

2   c – Known Change is not a specific term in ITIL.

3   d – All of the above statements are correct as stated in Section 6.4.

4   d – The full list of the activities in the Change Management process can be found in Section 6.5.2.

5   c – At the data level, the Configuration Management System may take data from several physical Configuration Management Databases, which together constitute a federated Configuration Management Database.

Service Operation

7

7 Service Operation

Guidance on achieving effectiveness and efficiency in the delivery and support of services so as to ensure value for the customer and the Service Provider.

Guidance on how to maintain stability in Service Operations, allowing for changes in design, scale, scope and service levels.

7.1 GOALS AND OBJECTIVES

The main goal is to achieve effectiveness and efficiency in the delivery and support of services and to maintain stability while at the same time allowing for changes and improvement.

The objectives of Service Operation are:

- to coordinate and carry out the activities and processes required to deliver and manage services at agreed levels to the business users and customers
- to manage the technology that is used to deliver and support services.

7.2 SCOPE

Service Operation includes the execution of all ongoing activities required to deliver and support services. The scope of Service Operation includes:

- **The services themselves** – any activity that forms part of a service is included in Service Operation, whether it is performed by the Service Provider, an external supplier or the user or customer of that service.

- **Service Management processes** – the ongoing management and execution of many Service Management processes are performed in Service Operation, even though a number of ITIL processes originate at the Service Design or Service Transition stage of the Service Lifecycle, they are in use continually in Service Operation.
- **Technology** – all services require some form of technology to deliver them. Managing this technology is not a separate issue, but an integral part of the management of the services themselves.
- **People** – regardless of what services, processes and technology are managed, they are all about people.

7.3 BUSINESS VALUE

Each stage in the Service Lifecycle provides value to business. For example, Service Value is modelled in Service Strategy, the cost of the service is designed, predicted and validated in Service Design and Service Transition, and measures for optimization are identified in CSI.

The operation of service is where these plans, designs and optimizations are executed and measured. From the customer's viewpoint, Service Operation is where actual value is seen.

7.4 KEY PRINCIPLES

7.4.1 Keeping the balance

Service Operation is more than just the repetitive execution of a standard set of procedures or activities. All functions, processes and activities are designed to deliver a specified and agreed level of services, but they have to be delivered in an ever-changing environment.

This forms a conflict between maintaining the status quo and adapting to changes in the business and technological environments (Figure 7.1).

Figure 7.1 A key role for Service Operation is to achieve a balance between conflicting sets of priorities

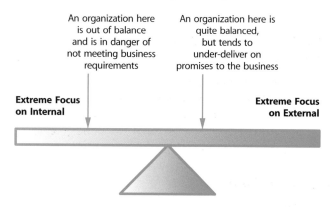

7.4.1.1 External versus internal focus

A fundamental conflict is between the view of IT as *a set of IT services* and the view of IT as a set of *technology components*.

- The *external view* is the way in which services are experienced by its users and customers. All they are concerned about is that the services are delivered as required and agreed.
- The *internal view* is the way in which IT components and systems are managed to deliver the services. Since IT systems are complex and diverse, this often means that the technology is managed by several different teams or departments – each of which is focused on achieving good performance and availability of 'their' systems.

Both views are necessary when delivering services. The organization that focuses only on business requirements without thinking about how it is going to deliver will end

up making promises that cannot be kept. The organization that focuses only on internal systems without thinking about what services it supports will end up with expensive services that deliver little value.

7.4.1.2 Stability versus responsiveness

No matter how good the functionality is of an IT service and no matter how well it has been designed, it will be of no worth if it is not available.

- **Stability** – This means that Service Operation needs to ensure that the IT Infrastructure is stable and available as designed.
- **Responsiveness** – At the same time Service Operation needs to recognize that business and IT requirements change. Each change brings with it an opportunity to provide better levels of service to the business. The ability to respond to change without impacting on other services is a significant challenge.

7.4.1.3 Quality versus cost

Service Operation is required to consistently deliver the agreed level of quality to its customers and users, while at the same time keeping costs and resource utilization at an optimal level.

An increase in the level of quality usually results in an increase in the cost of that service, and vice versa. However, the relationship is not always directly proportional.

Achieving an optimal balance between *cost* and *quality* is a key role of Service Management.

7.4.1.4 Reactive versus Proactive

Another balance exists between being reactive and proactive:

- A *reactive* organization is one which does not act unless it is prompted to do so by an external driver, e.g. a new business requirement, an application that has been developed, escalation in complaints made by users and customers.
- A *proactive* organization is always looking for ways to improve the current situation. It will continually scan the internal and external environments, looking for signs of potentially impacting changes.

Proactive behaviour is usually seen as positive, especially since it enables an organization to maintain competitive advantage in a changing environment. However, being too proactive can be expensive and can result in staff being distracted. The need for proper balance in reactive and proactive behaviour often achieves the optimal result.

7.4.2 Communication

Good communication is needed with other IT teams and departments, with users and internal customers, and between the Service Operation teams and departments themselves. Issues can often be prevented or mitigated with appropriate communication.

Types of communication include:

- routine operational communication
- communication between shifts
- Performance Reporting
- communication in projects
- communication related to changes
- communication related to exceptions and emergencies
- training of new or customized processes and Service Designs
- communication of strategy and design to Service Operation teams.

There is no definitive medium for communication, nor is there a fixed location or frequency. In some organizations communication has to take place in meetings. Other organizations prefer to use e-mail or the communication inherent in their Service Management tools.

7.5 PROCESSES

7.5.1 Event Management

7.5.1.1 Goals and objectives

- To provide a sound basis for Operational Monitoring and Control.
- To detect Events, make sense of them, and determine the appropriate control action.
- To act as a basis for automating routine Operations Management activities.

7.5.1.2 Basic concepts

Definition

An Event is a change of state which has significance for the management of the IT infrastructure or the delivery of an IT service.

Events are typically notifications created by an IT Service, CI or monitoring tool.

Definition

An Alert is a warning that a threshold has been reached, something has changed, or a failure has occurred.

There are many different types of Event:

Informational – Events that signify regular operation, such as:

- notification that a scheduled workload has been completed
- a user has logged in to an application
- an e-mail has reached its recipient.

Warning – Events that signify unusual, but not exceptional, operation. These are an indication that the situation may require closer monitoring. Examples of this type of Event are:

- a server's memory utilization reaches within 5% of its highest acceptable performance level
- the completion time of a transaction is 10% longer than normal.

Exception – Events that signify an exception include:

- a user attempting to log on to an application with an incorrect password
- a device's Central Processing Unit performing above the acceptable utilization rate
- a PC scan revealing the installation of unauthorized software.

7.5.1.3 Roles

Technical and Application Management teams play several important roles:

- During Service Design, these teams will participate in the instrumentation of the service, classify Events, update correlation engines, and ensure that any auto responses are defined.
- During Service Transition these teams will test the service to ensure that Events are properly generated and that the defined responses are appropriate.
- During Service Operation these teams will typically perform Event Management for the systems under their control.

Where IT Operations is separated from Technical or Application Management, it is common for Event Monitoring and first-line response to be delegated to IT Operations Management.

Operators for each area will be tasked with monitoring Events, responding as required, or ensuring that Incidents are created as appropriate.

7.5.2 Incident Management

7.5.2.1 Goals and objectives

- To restore normal Service Operation as quickly as possible and minimize the adverse impact on business operations.
- To ensure that the best possible levels of service quality and availability are maintained.

'Normal Service Operation' is defined here as Service Operation within SLA limits.

7.5.2.2 Scope

Incident Management includes any Event which disrupts, or which could disrupt, a service.

This includes Events which are:

- communicated directly by users, through the Service Desk
- communicated through an interface from Event Management to Incident Management
- reported or logged by technical staff.

This does not mean, however, that all Events are Incidents. Many classes of Event are not related to disruptions at all, but are indicators of normal operation or are simply informational.

7.5.2.3 Basic concepts

Definition

An Incident is an unplanned interruption to an IT service or reduction in the quality of an IT service. Failure of a CI that has not yet impacted on service is also an Incident.

In some cases it may be possible to find a Workaround to an Incident – a temporary way of overcoming the difficulties. But it is important that work on a permanent resolution continues where this is justified.

Definition

A Workaround is a means to reducing or eliminating the impact of an Incident or Problem for which a full resolution is not yet available.

Examples would be restarting a failed CI or making a manual amendment to an input file to allow a program to complete its run successfully.

Workarounds for Problems are documented in Known Error Records. Workarounds for Incidents that do not have associated Problem Records are documented in the Incident Record.

An important aspect of logging every Incident is to agree and allocate an appropriate priority – as this will determine how the Incident is handled both by support tools and support staff.

Prioritization can usually be determined by taking into account both the urgency of the Incident (how quickly the business needs a resolution), and the level of impact it is causing.

An effective way of calculating these elements and deriving an overall priority level for each Incident is shown in Figure 7.2.

An indication of *impact* is often the number of users being affected. However, in some cases the loss of service to a single user can have a major business impact so numbers alone are not enough to evaluate overall priority. Other factors that can also contribute to impact levels are:

- risk to life or limb
- number of services affected – may be multiple services
- level of financial losses
- effect on business reputation
- regulatory or legislative breaches.

Timescales must be agreed for all Incident handling stages depending on the priority level of the Incident – based on the overall Incident response and resolution targets within SLAs – and captured as targets within OLAs and Underpinning Contracts. All support groups should be made fully aware of these timescales.

A separate procedure, with shorter timescales and greater urgency, must be used for major Incidents. A definition of what constitutes a *major Incident* must be agreed and ideally mapped on to the overall Incident prioritization system – such that it will be dealt with through the major Incident process.

Many Incidents are not new. They involve dealing with something that has happened before and may well happen again. For this reason, some organizations find it helpful to predefine Incident Models.

Definition

An Incident Model is a way of predefining the steps that should be taken to handle a process for dealing with a particular type of Incident in an agreed way.

7.5.2.4 Process activities

The key activities within the Incident Management process include (Figure 7.3):

- **Incident identification:** Work cannot begin on dealing with an Incident until it is known that an Incident has occurred. Ideally Incidents should be resolved before they have an impact on users.
- **Incident logging:** All Incidents must be fully logged and date/time stamped, regardless of whether they are raised through a Service Desk telephone call or whether automatically detected via an Event Alert.
- **Incident categorization:** Part of the initial logging must be to allocate suitable Incident Categorization coding so that the exact type of the call is recorded.

Figure 7.2 Calculating the priority based on impact and urgency

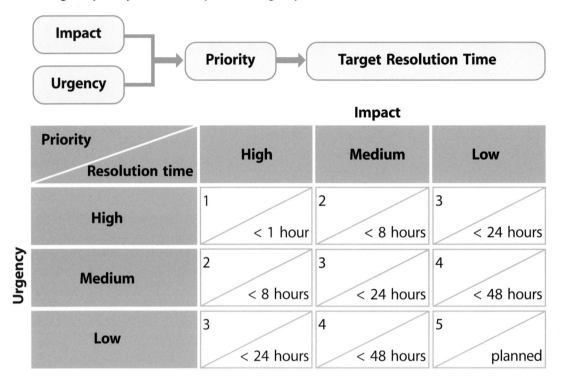

Priority / Resolution time	Impact		
	High	**Medium**	**Low**
High	1 / < 1 hour	2 / < 8 hours	3 / < 24 hours
Medium	2 / < 8 hours	3 / < 24 hours	4 / < 48 hours
Low	3 / < 24 hours	4 / < 48 hours	5 / planned

- **Incident prioritization:** An appropriate prioritization code must be agreed and allocated – as this will determine how the Incident is handled both by support tools and support staff. Prioritization can usually be determined by taking into account both the *urgency* of the Incident and the level of *impact* it is causing.

- **Initial diagnosis:** If the Incident has been routed via the Service Desk, the Service Desk Operator must carry out initial diagnosis, typically while the user is still on the telephone.

- **Incident escalation:**
  - **functional escalation** – as soon as it becomes clear that the Service Desk is unable to resolve the Incident itself or when target times for first point resolution have been exceeded, the Incident must be immediately escalated for further support
  - **hierarchic escalation** – if Incidents are of a serious nature (e.g. priority 1 Incidents) the appropriate IT managers must be notified, for informational purposes at least.
- **Investigation and diagnosis:** Each of the support groups involved with the Incident handling will investigate and diagnose what has gone wrong.

Figure 7.3 Incident Management process flow

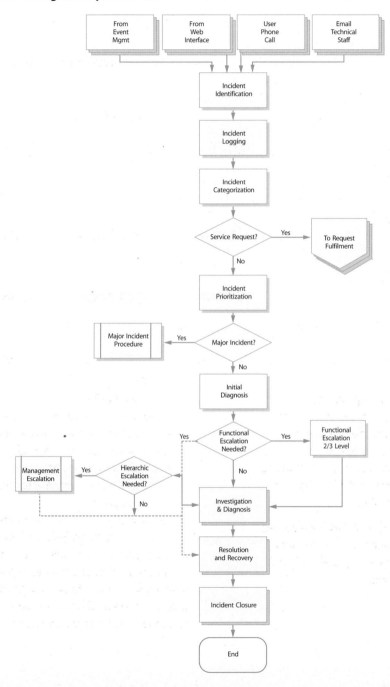

■ **Resolution and recovery:** When a potential resolution has been identified, this should be applied and tested.

■ **Incident closure:** The Service Desk should check that the Incident is fully resolved and that the users are satisfied and willing to agree the Incident can be closed.

7.5.2.5 Key metrics

The metrics that should be monitored and reported on to judge the efficiency and effectiveness of the Incident Management process, and its operation, may include:

■ total numbers of Incidents
■ breakdown of Incidents at each stage
■ size of current Incident backlog
■ number of major Incidents
■ mean elapsed time to achieve Incident resolution or circumvention, broken down by impact code
■ Percentage of Incidents handled within agreed response time.

7.5.2.6 Roles

An Incident Manager has the responsibility for:

■ driving the efficiency and effectiveness of the Incident Management process
■ producing management information
■ managing the work of Incident support staff (first- and second-line)
■ monitoring the effectiveness of Incident Management and making recommendations for improvement
■ developing and maintaining the Incident Management systems
■ managing major Incidents.

First-line support

See the Service Desk Function below.

Second-line support

Many organizations choose to have a second-line support group, made up of staff with greater (though still general) technical skills than the Service Desk – and with additional time to devote to Incident diagnosis and resolution without interference from telephone interruptions.

Third-line support

Third-line support is provided by a number of internal technical groups and/or third-party suppliers/maintainers.

7.5.2.7 Challenges

Typical challenges faced by Incident Management are:

■ detection of Incidents as early as possible
■ convincing all staff (technical teams as well as users) that all Incidents must be logged, and encouraging the use of self-help web-based capabilities
■ availability of information about Problems and Known Errors. This will enable Incident Management staff to learn from previous Incidents and also to track the status of resolutions
■ integration into the CMS to determine relationships between CIs, and to refer to the history of CIs when performing first-line support
■ integration into the Service Level Management process.

7.5.3 Request Fulfilment

7.5.3.1 Goals and objectives

■ To provide a channel for users to request and receive standard services for which a predefined approval and qualification process exists.

- To provide information to users and customers about the availability of services and the procedure for obtaining them.
- To source and deliver the components of requested standard services.

7.5.3.2 Basic concepts

> **Definition**
> A Service Request is a request from a user for information, or advice, or for a Standard Change or for access to an IT service.

The term Service Request is used as a generic description for the many varying types of demand that are placed on the IT department by users. Many of these are actually small changes – low risk, frequently occurring, low cost etc. (e.g. a request to change a password, a request to install an additional software application onto a particular workstation, a request to relocate some items of desktop equipment) – or they may be just a question requesting information.

Many Service Requests will frequently recur, so a predefined Request Model can be devised to include the stages needed to fulfil the request, the individuals or support groups involved, target timescales and escalation paths.

The need for a *Request Model* can often be satisfied by implementing a *Standard Change*. The ownership of Service Requests resides with the Service Desk, which monitors, escalates, dispatches and often fulfils the user's request.

7.5.3.3 Roles

Initial handling of Service Requests will be undertaken by the Service Desk and Incident Management staff.

Eventual fulfilment of the request will be undertaken by the appropriate Service Operation team(s) or departments or by external suppliers, as appropriate. Often Facilities Management, Procurement and other business areas aid in the fulfilment of the Service Request.

7.5.4 Problem Management

7.5.4.1 Goals and objectives

- To prevent Incidents and resulting Problems from happening, and to eliminate recurring Incidents.
- To minimize the impact of Incidents that cannot be prevented.

7.5.4.2 Basic concepts

> **Definition**
> A Problem is the unknown cause of one or more Incidents.

> **Definition**
> A Known Error is a Problem that has a documented root cause and a Workaround.

As soon as the diagnosis is complete, and particularly where a Workaround has been found, a Known Error record must be raised and placed in the Known Error Database – so that if further Incidents or problems arise they can be identified and the service restored more quickly.

However, in some cases it may be advantageous to raise a Known Error record even earlier in the overall process, for example just for information purposes, even though the diagnosis may not be complete or a Workaround found. So it is inadvisable to set a concrete procedural point exactly when a Known Error Record must be raised. It should be done as soon as it becomes useful to do so.

Definition

A resolution is an action taken to repair the root cause of an Incident or Problem, or to implement a Workaround.

Ideally, as soon as a solution has been found it should be applied to resolve the problem. However, in reality safeguards may be needed to ensure that this does not cause other difficulties.

If any change in functionality is required, this will require an RFC to be raised and approved before the resolution can be applied.

To allow quicker diagnosis and resolution of Incidents and Problems, previous knowledge of how they were overcome should be stored in a *Known Error Database*.

Many Problems will be unique and will require handling in an individual way. However, it is conceivable that some Incidents may recur because of dormant or underlying Problems.

Besides the creation of a Known Error Record in the Known Error Database to ensure quicker diagnosis, the creation of a *Problem Model* for handling such problems in the future may be helpful.

7.5.4.3 Roles

The Problem Manager has responsibility for ensuring that the aims of Problem Management are met. This includes such responsibilities as:

- liaising with all Problem resolution groups to ensure swift resolution of problems within the SLA targets
- ownership and protection of the Known Error Database
- formal closure of all Problem Records

- liaising with suppliers, contractors, etc. to ensure that third parties fulfil their contractual obligations, especially with regard to resolving problems and providing problem-related information and data
- arranging, running, documenting and all follow-up activities relating to major Problem Reviews.

7.5.4.4 Problem-solving groups

The actual solving of problems is likely to be undertaken by one or more technical support groups and/or suppliers or support contractors, under the coordination of the Problem Manager.

7.5.5 Access Management

7.5.5.1 Goals and objectives

- To provide the right for users to be able to use a service or group of services.
- To execute policies and actions defined in Security and Availability Management.

7.5.5.2 Basic concepts

Access Management is the process that enables users to use the services that are documented in the Service Catalogue. It comprises the following basic concepts.

Definition

Access refers to the level and extent of a service's functionality or data that a user is entitled to use.

Definition

Identity refers to a unique name that is used to identify a user, person or role. The identity is used to grant rights to that user, person or role.

Definition

Rights (also called privileges) are entitlements, or permissions, granted to a user or role.

Rights refer to the actual settings whereby a user is provided access to a service or group of services. Typical rights, or levels of access, are: read, write, execute, change and delete.

7.5.5.3 Roles

The Service Desk is typically used as a means to request access to a service. This is usually done using a Service Request. The Service Desk will validate the request by checking that the request has been approved at the appropriate level of authority, that the user is a legitimate employee, contractor or customer and that they qualify for access.

The Service Desk will then pass the request to the appropriate team to provide access. It is quite common for the Service Desk to be delegated responsibility for providing access for simple services during the call.

Technical and Application Management teams play several important roles:

- During Service Design, these teams will ensure that mechanisms are created to simplify and control Access Management on each service that is designed. They will also specify ways in which misuse of rights can be detected and stopped.
- During Service Transition these teams will test the service to ensure that access can be granted, controlled and prevented as designed.
- During Service Operation these teams will typically perform Access Management for the systems under their control.

Where *IT Operations* is separated from Technical or Application Management, it is common for operational Access Management tasks to be delegated to IT Operations Management.

7.6 FUNCTIONS

7.6.1 Service Desk

7.6.1.1 Role

A Service Desk is a functional unit made up of a dedicated number of staff responsible for dealing with a variety of service Incidents and Events, often reported via telephone calls, web interface, or automatically reported infrastructure Events.

The Service Desk should be the *single point of contact* for IT users on a day-to-day basis for all Incidents and Service Requests.

The value of an effective Service Desk should not be underrated. A good Service Desk can compensate for deficiencies elsewhere in the IT organization, but a mediocre Service Desk can give a poor impression of an otherwise very effective IT organization.

7.6.1.2 Objectives

The primary objective of the Service Desk is to restore the 'normal service' to users as quickly as possible. While this can involve fixing a technical fault, it can equally involve fulfilling a Service Request or answering a query – anything that is needed to allow users to return to working satisfactorily.

Specific responsibilities of the Service Desk are:

- logging all relevant Incident/Service Request details, and allocating categorization and prioritization codes
- providing first-line investigation and diagnosis
- resolving the Incidents/Service requests they are able to

Figure 7.4 Local Service Desk

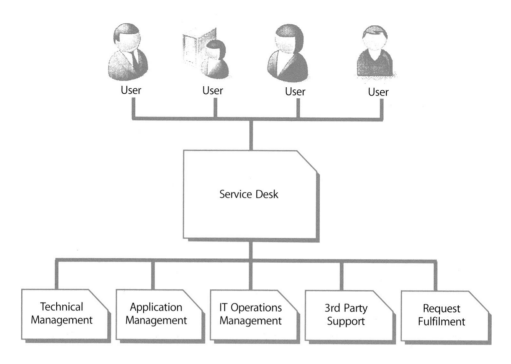

- escalating the Incidents/Service Requests that they cannot resolve within agreed timescales
- keeping users informed of progress
- closing all resolved Incidents, Requests and other calls
- conducting customer/user satisfaction call-backs/ surveys as agreed.

7.6.1.3 Organizational structures

There are many ways of structuring and locating Service Desks. The main options are:

- Local Service Desk
- Centralized Service Desk
- Virtual Service Desk
- Follow-the-Sun.

In reality, an organization may need to implement a structure that combines a number of these options to fully meet the business needs.

Local Service Desk

This is where a desk is co-located within or physically close to the user community it serves (Figure 7.4).

A local Service Desk often aids communication and gives a clearly visible presence which some users like. However, it can often be inefficient and expensive to resource as staff will be tied up waiting to deal with Incidents, when the volume and arrival rate of calls may not justify this.

Centralized Service Desk

It is possible to reduce the number of Service Desks by merging them into a single location (or into a smaller

Figure 7.5 Centralized Service Desk

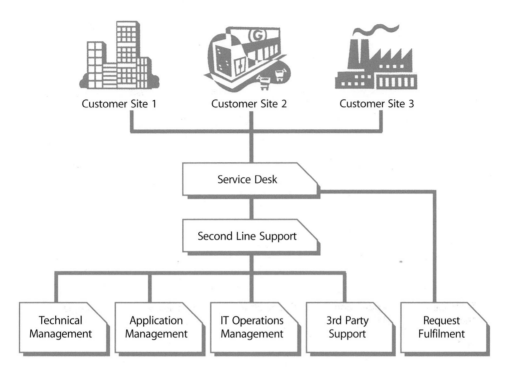

Customer Site 1   Customer Site 2   Customer Site 3

Service Desk

Second Line Support

| Technical Management | Application Management | IT Operations Management | 3rd Party Support | Request Fulfilment |

number of locations) by drawing the staff into one or more centralized Service Desk structures (Figure 7.5).

Centralized Service Desks can be more efficient and cost effective, allowing fewer overall staff to deal with a higher volume of calls. They can also lead to higher skill levels through great familiarization as a result of more frequent occurrence of Events.

Virtual Service Desk

Through the use of technology and corporate support tools, it is possible to give the impression of a single, centralized Service Desk when, in fact, the personnel may be spread or located in any number of geographical locations (Figure 7.6).

Virtual Service Desks bring in the option of 'home working', secondary support group, off-shoring or outsourcing, or any combination necessary to meet user demand.

Follow-the-sun

Some global organizations may wish to combine two or more of their geographically dispersed Service Desks to provide a 24-hour follow-the-sun service. For example, a Service Desk in Asia-Pacific may handle calls during its standard office hours, and at the end of this period they may hand over responsibility for any open Incidents to a European-based Service Desk. This can give 24-hour coverage at relatively low cost as no desk has to work more than a single shift.

Figure 7.6 Virtual Service Desk

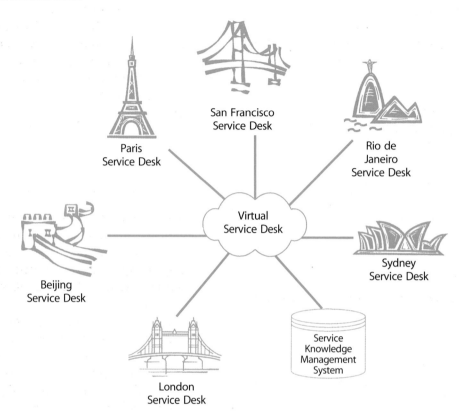

7.6.1.4 Staffing

Staffing levels

An organization must ensure that the correct number of staff is available at any given time to match the demand being placed on the Service Desk by the business. Statistical analysis of call arrival rates under current support arrangements must be undertaken and then closely monitored and adjusted as necessary.

Skill levels

A range of skill options are possible, starting from a 'call logging' service only – where staff need only very basic technical skills – right through to a 'technical' Service Desk – where an organization's most technically skilled staff are used.

The required skills include:

■ interpersonal skills
■ business awareness

- service awareness
- technical awareness
- diagnostic skills
- knowledge and use of support tools and techniques
- knowledge and use of processes and procedures.

Training

It is vital that all Service Desk staff are adequately trained before they are called on to staff the Service Desk. A formal induction programme should be undertaken by all new staff.

When starting, new staff should initially 'shadow' experienced staff; that is, they should sit with experienced staff and listen in on calls before starting to take calls themselves. When they do start taking calls, there should be a mentor listening in who will be able to intervene and provide support where necessary.

A programme will be necessary to keep the Service Desk staff's knowledge up to date.

Staff retention

Any significant loss of staff can be disruptive and lead to inconsistency of service. Therefore efforts should be made to make the Service Desk an attractive place to work.

Super users

Many organizations find it useful to appoint or designate a number of 'super users' throughout the user community to act as liaison points with IT in general and the Service Desk in particular.

7.6.1.5 Metrics

Service Desk metrics can include:

- customer and user satisfaction
- the first-line resolution rate
- average time to resolve an Incident (when resolved at first line)
- average time to escalate an Incident (where first-line resolution is not possible)
- average Service Desk cost of handling an Incident
- percentage of customer or user updates conducted within target times, as defined in SLA targets
- the number of calls broken down by time of day and day of week, combined with the average call time metric.

7.6.2 Technical Management

7.6.2.1 Role

Technical Management plays a dual role:

- It is the *custodian* of technical knowledge and expertise related to managing the IT infrastructure. In this role Technical Management ensures that the knowledge required to design, test, manage and improve IT services is identified, developed and refined.
- It provides the actual *resources* to support the IT Service Management Lifecycle. In this role Technical Management ensures that resources are effectively trained and deployed to design, build, transition, operate and improve the technology required to deliver and support IT services.

7.6.2.2 Objectives

The objectives of Technical Management are to help plan, implement and maintain a stable technical infrastructure to support the organization's business processes through:

- well designed and highly resilient, cost-effective technical topology
- use of adequate technical skills to maintain the technical infrastructure in optimum condition
- swift use of technical skills to speedily diagnose and resolve any technical failures that occur.

7.6.2.3 Overlap

The Technical Management function may overlap the IT Operations Management function because both functions play a role in management and maintenance of the IT infrastructure.

The Technical Management function may also overlap the Application Management function because both functions play an important role in the design, testing and improvement of CIs that form part of IT services.

7.6.3 IT Operations Management

7.6.3.1 Role

IT Operations Management is the function responsible for the ongoing management of an organization's IT infrastructure to ensure delivery of the agreed level of IT services.

The role of IT Operations Management is to execute the ongoing activities and procedures required to manage and maintain the IT infrastructure. These activities include:

- **Operations Control** – which oversees the execution and monitoring of the operational activities and events in the IT infrastructure. In addition, Operations Control also performs the following specific tasks:
  - console management
  - job scheduling
  - backup and restore
  - print and output management
  - performance of maintenance activities.
- **Facilities Management** – which refers to the management of the physical IT environment, typically a data centre or computer rooms and recovery sites together with the power and cooling equipment.

As with many IT Service Management processes and functions, IT Operations Management has a dual role:

- It is responsible for executing the activities and performance standards defined during Service Design and tested during Service Transition.
- At the same time it is part of the process of adding value to the different lines of business and to support the value network.

7.6.3.2 Objectives

- Maintenance of the 'status quo' to achieve stability of an organization's day-to-day processes and activities.
- Regular scrutiny and improvements to achieve improved service at reduced costs, while maintaining stability.
- Swift application of operational skills to diagnose and resolve any IT operations failures that occur.

7.6.3.3 Overlap

The IT Operations Management function may overlap the Technical Management function because both functions have a role in management and maintenance of the IT infrastructure.

The IT Operations Management function may overlap the Application Management function because both functions have a role in application support.

7.6.4 Applications Management

7.6.4.1 Role

Application Management is responsible for managing applications throughout their lifecycle. Application Management also has an important role in the design, testing and improvement of applications that form part of IT services. As such this team may be involved in development projects, but it is not usually the same as the Application Development team. One of the key decisions it contributes to is the decision of whether to buy or build an application.

Application Management has a dual role:

- It is the *custodian* of technical knowledge and expertise related to managing applications. In this role Application Management, working together with Technical Management, ensures that the knowledge required to design, test, manage and improve IT services is identified, developed and refined.
- It provides the actual resources to support the IT Service Management Lifecycle. In this role Application Management ensures that resources are effectively trained and deployed to design, build, transition, operate and improve the technology required to deliver and support IT services.

In addition to these two high-level roles, Application Management also performs the following two specific roles:

- It provides guidance to IT Operations about how best to carry out the ongoing operational management of applications.
- The integration of the Application Management Lifecycle into the IT Service Management Lifecycle.

7.6.4.2 Objectives

The objectives of Application Management are to support the organization's business processes by helping to identify functional and manageability requirements for application software, and then to assist in the design and deployment of those applications and to provide ongoing support and improvement of those applications.

These objectives are achieved through:

- applications that are well designed, resilient and cost effective
- ensuring that the required functionality is available to achieve the required business outcome
- assuring the organization of adequate technical skills to maintain operational applications in optimum condition
- swift use of technical skills to speedily diagnose and resolve any technical failures that occur.

7.6.4.3 Overlap

The Application Management function may overlap the Technical Management function because both functions have an important role in the design, testing and improvement of CIs that form part of IT Services.

The Application Management function may overlap the IT Operations Management function because both functions have a role in application support.

7.7 SAMPLE QUESTIONS AND ANSWERS

7.7.1 Questions

1 Which of the following statements BEST describes the objective of Service Operation?
   a To design services to satisfy business objectives.
   b To ensure that the service can be used in accordance with the requirements and constraints specified within the service requirements.
   c To achieve effectiveness and efficiency in the delivery and support of services.
   d To transform Service Management into a strategic asset.

2 Which of the following statements is the CORRECT definition of a Known Error?

   a An action taken to repair the root cause of an Incident or Problem.

   b A Problem that has a documented root cause or a Workaround.

   c The unknown cause of one or more Incidents.

   d A Problem that has a documented root cause and a Workaround.

3 Which of the following balances has to be dealt with by Service Operation?

   a Supply versus demand

   b Push versus pull

   c Stability versus responsiveness

   d Cost versus resources

4 Which of the following activities is NOT an activity in the Incident Management process?

   a Incident Identification

   b Incident Verification

   c Incident Categorization

   d Incident Prioritization

5 Which of the following activities is the Incident Manager responsible for?

   1 Producing management information.

   2 Monitoring the effectiveness of Incident Management and making recommendations for improvement.

   3 Managing the work of Incident support staff (first-line and second-line).

   4 Managing major Incidents.

   a 1 only

   b 2 and 3 only

   c 1, 2 and 4 only

   d All of the above.

6 Which of the following is an objective for Problem Management?

   a To define, document, agree, monitor, measure, report and review the level of IT services provided.

   b To minimize the impact of Incidents that cannot be prevented.

   c To restore normal Service Operation as quickly as possible and minimize the adverse impact on business operations.

   d To act as a basis for automating routine Operations Management activities.

7 Which of the following are examples of Event types?

   1 Informational

   2 Warning

   3 Major

   4 Exception.

   a 2 only

   b 2 and 4 only

   c 1, 2 and 4 only

   d All of the above.

8 Which of the following options are typical ways of structuring and locating a Service Desk?

   1 Local Service Desk

   2 Centralized Service Desk

   3 Virtual Service Desk

   4 Follow-the-Sun

   a 1 only

   b 1 and 2 only

   c 1, 2 and 3 only

   d All of the above.

9 Which of the following is NOT a responsibility of a Service Desk?

   a Providing first-line investigation and diagnosis.

   b Closing all resolved Incidents.

   c Resolving those Incidents it is able to resolve.

   d Closing all resolved Known Errors.

10 Which of the following is NOT described as a function but as a process in Service Operation?

a   Event Management
b   Applications Management
c   IT Operations Management
d   Technical Management.

7.7.2 Answers

1   c – Option (a) is an objective of Service Design, option (b) is an objective of Service Transition and option (d) is an objective of Service Strategy.

2   d – Option (a) is the definition of a resolution, option (b) does not reflect that the definition of a Known Error requires both a root cause and a Workaround, and option (c) is the definition of a Problem.

3   c – Options (a) and (d) are dealt with by Capacity Management in Service Design and option (b) refers to two alternative ways of deployment in Service Transition.

4   b – Incident verification is not an activity in the Incident Management process.

5   d – All the activities are part of the responsibilities of the Incident Manager.

6   b – Option (a) is an objective for Service Level Management. Option (c) is an objective for Incident Management and option (d) is an objective for Event Management.

7   c – 'Major' is not a type of Event but a 'type' of Incident.

8   d – All of the options can be used to structure and locate a Service Desk. In reality, an organization may need to implement a structure that combines a number of these options to fully meet the business needs.

9   d – Closing all resolved Known Errors is a responsibility of Problem Management.

10 a

Continual Service Improvement

8

8 Continual Service Improvement

Guidance in creating and maintaining value for customers through better design, introduction, and operation of services.

Guidance in realizing incremental and large-scale improvements in service quality, operational efficiency and business continuity.

Guidance in linking improvement efforts and outcomes with Service Strategy, Service Design and Service Transition.

8.1 GOALS AND OBJECTIVES

The primary goal of CSI is to continually align and realign IT services to the changing business needs by identifying and implementing improvements to IT services that support business processes. In effect, CSI is about looking for ways to improve process effectiveness and efficiency as well as cost effectiveness.

The objectives of CSI include:

- to review, analyse and make recommendations on improvement opportunities in each lifecycle phase
- to review and analyse Service Level Achievement results
- to identify and implement individual activities in order to improve service quality and improve the efficiency and effectiveness of enabling Service Management processes
- to improve cost effectiveness of delivering services without sacrificing customer satisfaction
- to ensure applicable quality management methods are used to support continual improvement activities.

8.2 SCOPE

CSI needs to address three main areas:

1 the overall health of Service Management as a discipline
2 the continual alignment of the portfolio of services with the current and future business needs
3 the maturity of the enabling processes for each service in a continual Service Lifecycle model.

8.3 BUSINESS VALUE

There are two commonly used terms when discussing Service Improvement outcomes:

- **Improvements:** Outcomes that when compared to the 'before' state, show a measurable increase in a desirable metric or decrease in an undesirable metric.
- **Benefits:** The gains achieved through realization of improvements, usually but not always expressed in monetary terms.

8.4 KEY PRINCIPLES

8.4.1 IT governance

Definition

IT Governance is the responsibility of the Board of Directors and executive management. It is an integral part of enterprise governance and consists of the leadership and organizational structures and processes that ensure that the organization's IT sustains and extends the organization's strategy and objectives.

IT Governance Institute (2001)

Figure 8.1 The Deming Cycle

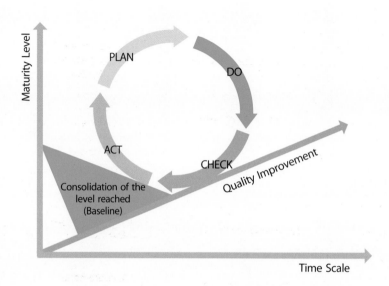

IT governance touches nearly every area of CSI. On one hand, IT must comply with new rules and legislation and continually demonstrate compliance through successful independent audits by external organizations. On the other hand, IT is increasingly being called upon to 'do more with less' and create additional value while maximizing the use of existing resources.

These increasing pressures fit perfectly together with the basic premise of ITIL: IT is a service business. Existing internal IT organizations must transform themselves into effective and efficient IT Service Providers or they will cease to be relevant to the business and, soon after, cease to exist. This continual and unceasing drive towards greater business value with greater internal efficiency is at the heart of CSI.

8.4.2 Deming Cycle

W Edwards Deming is well known for proposing the Deming Cycle for quality improvement. The four key stages of the cycle are 'Plan, Do, Check, Act' (PDCA), after which a phase of consolidation prevents the cycle from rolling back down the hill (Figure 8.1). Our goal in using the Deming Cycle is steady, ongoing improvement. It is a fundamental tenet of CSI.

Planning for improvement initiatives (Plan)

At this stage goals and measures for success are established, a gap analysis is performed, action steps to close the gap are defined, and measures to ensure the gap was closed are established and implemented.

Implementation of improvement initiative (Do)

This includes development and implementation of a project to close the identified gaps, implementation of

Figure 8.2 Continual Service Improvement model

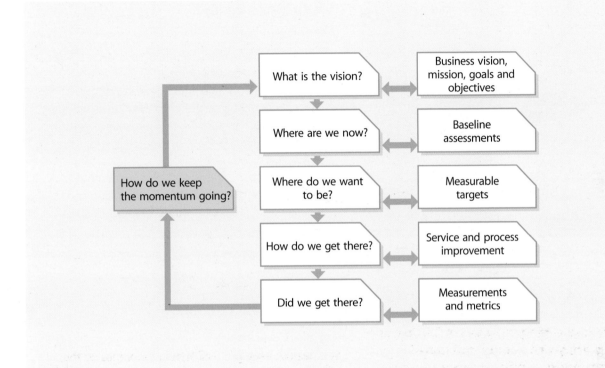

the improvement to Service Management processes, and establishment of the smooth operation of the process.

Monitor, measure and review services and Service Management processes (Check)

During this stage the implemented improvements are compared with the measures of success established in the Plan phase.

Continual service and Service Management process improvement (Act)

This stage requires implementing the actual service and Service Management process improvements. A decision to keep the status quo, close the gap or add necessary

resources needs to be made to determine whether further work is required to close remaining gaps and whether allocation of resources is necessary to support another round of improvement. Project decisions at this stage are the input for the next round of the PDCA cycle, closing the loop as input in the next Plan stage.

8.4.3 The Continual Service Improvement model

The CSI model (Figure 8.2) is an example of the Deming Cycle.

The model illustrates the constant cycle for improvement. The improvement process can be summarized in six steps:

Figure 8.3 Why do we measure?

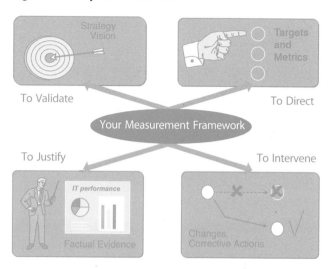

1 embracing the *vision* by understanding the high-level business objectives

2 assessing the *current situation* to obtain an accurate, unbiased snapshot of where the organization is right now

3 understanding and agreeing on the priorities for improvement based on a deeper development of the principles defined in the vision. The full vision may be years away but this step provides *specific goals* and *a manageable timeframe*

4 detailing the CSI plan to achieve higher-quality service provision by *developing and implementing* IT Service Management processes

5 verifying that *measurements and metrics* are in place to ensure that milestones were achieved, process compliance is high, and business objectives and priorities were met by the level of service

6 finally, ensuring that the *momentum* for quality improvement is maintained by assuring that changes become embedded in the organization.

8.4.4 Measurement

8.4.4.1 Why measure?

Measurement is done (Figure 8.3):

■ to validate – monitoring and measuring to validate previous decisions.

■ to direct – monitoring and measuring to set direction for activities in order to meet set targets.

■ to justify – monitoring and measuring to justify, with factual evidence or proof, that a course of action is required.

■ to intervene – monitoring and measuring to identify a point of intervention, including subsequent changes and corrective actions.

The four basic reasons to monitor and measure lead to three key questions:

■ Why are we monitoring and measuring?

■ When do we stop?

■ Is anyone using the data?

Too often, we continue to measure long after the need has passed. Every time you produce a report you should ask: 'Do we still need this?'

8.4.4.2 Baselines

An important starting point for highlighting improvement is to establish baselines as markers or starting points for later comparison. Baselines are also used to establish an initial data point to determine if a service or process needs to be improved.

If a baseline is not initially established, the first measurement efforts will become the baseline. This is why it is essential to collect data at the outset, even if the integrity of the data is in question. It is better to have data to question than to have no data at all.

Figure 8.4 The DIKW (data, information, knowledge and wisdom) model

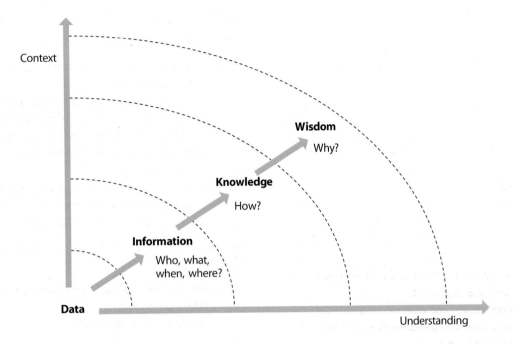

8.4.4.3 Types of metrics

It is important to remember that there are three types of metrics that an organization will need to collect to support CSI activities.

Technology metrics

These metrics are often associated with component-based and application-based metrics, such as performance, availability etc.

Process metrics

These metrics are captured in the form of critical success factors (CSFs), KPIs and activity metrics for the Service Management processes. These metrics can help determine the overall health of a process. Four key questions that KPIs can help answer are around quality, performance, value and compliance of following the process. CSI uses these metrics as input in identifying improvement opportunities for each process.

Service Metrics

These metrics are the results of the end-to-end service. Component metrics are used to compute the Service Metrics.

8.5 PROCESSES

8.5.1 The 7-Step Improvement Process

8.5.1.1 Goals and objectives

- To identify goals and objectives to properly identify what should be measured.

Figure 8.5 From vision to measurements

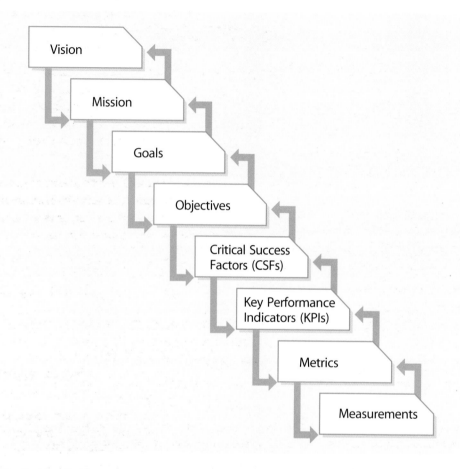

- To identify the measurements that can be provided based on existing toolsets, organizational culture and process maturity.
- To review and analyse data to convert the data in the required format and for the required audience, and to transform the information into knowledge of the Events that are affecting the organization.
- To identify and implement individual activities to improve service quality and improve the efficiency and effectiveness of enabling Service Management processes.

8.5.1.2 Basic concepts

Service Analytics involves analysis to produce knowledge and synthesis to provide understanding.

Data to wisdom (Figure 8.4)

Data is quantitative. It is defined as numbers, characters, images or other outputs from devices to convert physical quantities into symbols in a very broad sense.

Information is defined as a message received and understood. Information is the result of processing and

Figure 8.6 The 7-Step Improvement Process

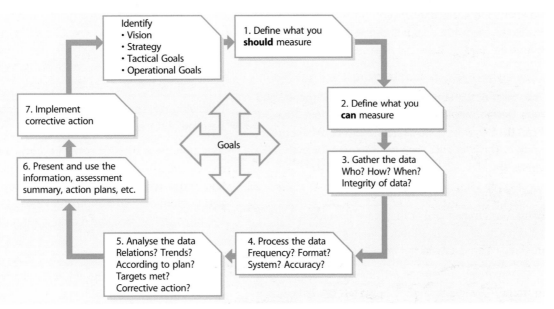

organizing data in a way that adds to the knowledge of the person receiving it.

Knowledge can be defined as information combined with experience, context, interpretation and reflection.

Wisdom is defined as the ability to make correct judgements and decisions. It consists of making the best use of available knowledge.

Vision to measurements (Figure 8.5)

A *Vision* is a description of what an organization intends to become in the future.

The *Mission Statement* of an organization is a short but complete description of the overall purpose and intentions of that organization. It states what is to be achieved, but not how this should be done.

A *Goal* is a means to help us to decide on a course of action.

The *Objective* is the defined purpose or aim of a process, an activity or an organization as a whole. Objectives are usually expressed as measurable targets.

A *CSF* is something that must happen if a process, project, plan or service is to succeed.

A *KPI* is a metric that is used to help manage a process, service or activity. Many metrics may be measured, but only the most important of these are defined as KPIs and used to actively manage and report on the process, service or activity. KPIs are used to measure the achievement of each CSF. For example a CSF of 'protect IT services when making changes' could be measured by KPIs such as 'percentage reduction of unsuccessful changes', 'percentage reduction in changes causing Incidents' etc.

A *metric* is something that is measured and reported to help manage a process, service or activity. In general, a metric is a scale of *measurement* defined in terms of a standard, i.e. in terms of a well-defined unit.

8.5.1.3 Process activities

Fundamental to CSI is the concept of measurement. CSI uses the following 7-Step Improvement Process (Figure 8.6).

1 Define what you should measure

At the onset of the Service Lifecycle, Service Strategy and Service Design should have identified this information. CSI can then start its cycle all over again at 'Where are we now?'. This identifies the ideal situation for both the business and IT.

2 Define what you can measure

Organizations may find that they have limitations on what can actually be measured. If you cannot measure something, then it should not appear in an SLA.

This activity relates to the CSI activities of 'Where do we want to be?'. By identifying the new SLRs of the business, the IT capabilities and the available budgets, CSI can conduct a gap analysis to identify the opportunities for improvement as well as answering the question 'How will we get there?'

3–5 Gathering, processing and analysing the data

In order to properly answer the 'Did we get there?' question, data must first be gathered, processed and analysed. Data is gathered based on the vision, mission, goals and objectives. Data processing, aligned with CSFs and KPIs, takes place before the information is analysed to identify gaps and trends, along with reasons, before it is presented to the business.

6 Presenting and using the information

Here the answer to 'Did we get there?' is formatted and communicated in a such way as to present to the various stakeholders an accurate picture of the results of the improvement efforts. Knowledge is presented to the business in a form and manner that reflects its needs and assists the business in determining the next steps.

7 Implementing corrective action

In this step, the knowledge gained is used to optimize, improve and correct services. Managers identify issues and present solutions. The corrective actions that need to be taken to improve the service are communicated and explained to the organization.

Following this step, the organization establishes a new baseline and the cycle begins anew.

Although these seven steps of improvement appear to form a circular set of activities, they in fact constitute a knowledge spiral. In actual practice, knowledge gathered and wisdom derived from that knowledge at one level of the organization become a data input to the next.

8.5.1.4 Key metrics

There are two basic kinds of KPI: qualitative and quantitative.

A qualitative example

- CSF: improving IT service quality.
- KPI: a 10% increase in customer satisfaction rating for handling Incidents over the next six months.
- Metrics required:
  - original customer satisfaction score for handling Incidents
  - ending customer satisfaction score for handling Incidents.
- Measurements:
  - Incident handling survey score
  - number of survey scores.

A quantitative example

- CSF: reducing IT costs.
- KPI: a 10% reduction in the costs of handling printer Incidents.
- Metrics required:
  - original cost of handling printer Incidents
  - ending cost of handling printer Incidents.

- Cost of the improvement effort.
- Measurements:
  - time spent on the Incident by first-level and second-level operatives and their average salary
  - time spent on Problem Management activities by the second-level operative and their average salary
  - time spent on training the first-level operative on the Workaround
  - cost of a service call to third-party vendor
  - time and material from third-party vendor.

8.5.1.5 Roles

The Service Manager is responsible for the full lifecycle management of services. This includes responsibilities such as:

- providing leadership on the development of the Business Case and product-line strategy and architecture, new service deployment and lifecycle management schedules
- performing Service Cost Management activities in close partnership with other organizations such as Operations, Engineering and Finance
- instilling a market focus
- creating an organization which encourages high performance and innovative contributions from its members within a rapidly changing environment.

The CSI Manager is ultimately responsible for the success of all improvement activities. This includes responsibilities such as:

- developing the CSI domain
- ensuring that CSI roles have been filled
- working with the Service Owner to identify and prioritize improvement opportunities
- working with the Service Level Manager to ensure that monitoring requirements are defined and Service Improvement Programmes are identified

- ensuring that monitoring tools are in place to gather data
- ensuring baseline data is captured to measure improvement against
- defining and reporting on CSI CSFs, KPIs and activity metrics.
- helping prioritize improvement opportunities.

Other CSI roles are:

- Service Owner
- Service Level Manager
- Process owner
- Process managers
- Customers
- Senior IT managers
- Internal and external providers
- Individuals involved in day-to-day process activities within the Service Transition and Service Operations lifecycle phases
- Individuals involved with providing the service.

8.6 SAMPLE QUESTIONS AND ANSWERS

8.6.1 Questions

1 Which of the following is NOT an activity in the Deming PDCA cycle?
  a Plan
  b Do
  c Check
  d Align

2 What are the reasons to monitor and measure?
  1 To validate – monitoring and measuring to validate previous decisions.
  2 To direct – monitoring and measuring to set direction for activities in order to meet set targets.

3　To justify – monitoring and measuring to justify, with factual evidence or proof, that a course of action is required.

4　To intervene – monitoring and measuring to identify a point of intervention, including subsequent changes and corrective actions.

a　1 only

b　1 and 2 only

c　1, 2 and 4 only

d　All of the above.

3　Which of the following is an objective for the 7-Step Improvement Process?

a　To provide operational visibility, insight and superior decision making.

b　To design processes for the design, transition, operation and improvement of IT services.

c　To identify goals and objectives in order to properly identify what should be measured.

d　To minimize the impact of Incidents that cannot be prevented.

8.6.2 Answers

1　d – The activities in PDCA are Plan, Do, Check and Act.

2　d – All the options are basic reasons to monitor and measure.

3　c – Option (a) is an objective for Financial Management, (b) is an objective for Service Design, and (d) is an objective for Problem Management.

Service Management Technology

9   Service Management Technology

Technology has a major role in Service Management and this should be designed in, and mechanisms for maintaining and maximizing benefit from that technology must be in place.

9.1   USE OF TECHNOLOGY

Service Management is supported by technology in two ways:

- enterprise-wide tools that support the broader systems and processes within IT Service Management

- tools targeted more specifically at supporting an IT Service Management lifecycle phase or parts of a phase.

Service Management Technology enables the communication between Service Providers and customers. There are five modes in which technology interacts with a Service Provider's customers (Figure 9.1):

- Technology-free – technology is not involved in the service encounter.
- Technology-assisted – a service encounter in which only the Service Provider has access to the technology.

Figure 9.1 Types of service technology encounters

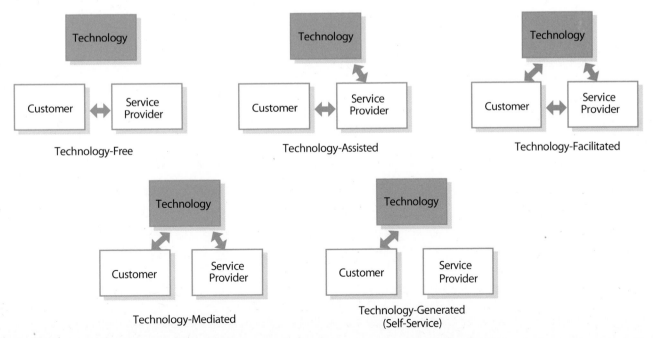

- Technology-facilitated – a service encounter in which both the Service Provider and the customer have access to the same technology.
- Technology-mediated – a service encounter in which the Service Provider and the customer are not in physical proximity.
- Technology-generated – a service encounter in which the Service Provider is represented entirely by technology, commonly known as self-service.

The tools and techniques are many and varied, including both proprietary and non-proprietary, and are beneficial in:

- speeding up the Service Management processes
- ensuring that standards and conventions are followed
- offering prototyping, modelling and simulation facilities
- enabling 'What if?' scenarios to be examined
- enabling interfaces and dependencies to be checked and correlated.

9.2 GENERIC REQUIREMENTS

An integrated Service Management technology that includes the following core functionality is needed.

9.2.1 Support and assistance for all stages in the Service Lifecycle

The Service Management tools should support the management of:

- all aspects of the service and its performance
- service achievement, the SLA, the OLA, contractual and supplier measurement, reporting and management
- consolidated metrics and metrics trees, with views from management dashboards down to detailed component information, performance, and fault analysis and identification

- consistent and consolidated views across all processes, systems, technologies and groups
- relationships and integration of the business and its processes with IT services, systems and processes
- a comprehensive set of search, data mining and reporting facilities, enabling accurate information and analysis for informed decision making
- service costs
- relationships, interfaces and interdependencies
- the Service Portfolio and Service Catalogue
- a Service Knowledge Management System.

9.2.2 Service Design tools

Many tools and techniques can be used to assist with the design of services and their associated components. These tools enable:

- hardware design
- software design
- environmental design
- process design
- data design.

9.2.3 Self-help capabilities

Many organizations find it beneficial to offer self-help capabilities to their users. The technology should therefore support this capability with some form of front end allowing the offering of a menu-driven range of self-help and Service Requests – with a direct interface into the back-end process handling software.

9.2.4 Workflow or process engine

A workflow or process control engine is needed to allow the pre-definition and control of defined processes such as an Incident Lifecycle, Request Fulfilment Lifecycle, Problem Lifecycle, Change model etc.

9.2.5 Integrated Configuration Management System

The tool should have an integrated CMS to allow an organization's IT infrastructure assets, components, services and any additional CIs to be held, together with all relevant attributes, in a centralized location. It should also allow relationships between each to be stored and maintained, and linked to Incident, Problem, Known Error and Change records as appropriate.

9.2.6 Discovery/deployment/licensing technology

In order to populate or verify the CMS data and to assist in Licence Management, discovery or automated audit tools will be required. Such tools should be capable of being run from any location on the network and allow interrogation and recovery of information relating to all components that make up, or are connected to, the IT infrastructure.

9.2.7 Remote control

It is often helpful for the Service Desk analysts and other support groups to be able to take control of the user's desktop.

9.2.8 Diagnostic utilities

It is extremely useful for Service Desk and other support groups if the technology incorporates the capability to create and use diagnostic scripts and other diagnostic utilities (such as, for example, case-based reasoning tools) to assist with early diagnosis of Incidents. Ideally these should be 'context sensitive' and presentation of the scripts automated as far as possible.

9.2.9 Reporting

There is no use storing data unless it can be easily retrieved and used to meet an organization's purposes. The technology should therefore incorporate good reporting capabilities and allow standard interfaces which can be used to input data to industry-standard reporting packages, dashboards etc.

9.2.10 Dashboards

Dashboard-type technology is useful to allow 'see at a glance' visibility of overall IT service performance and availability levels.

9.2.11 Integration with Business Service Management

There is a trend within the IT industry to try to bring together business-related IT with the processes and disciplines of IT Service Management – some call this Business Service Management. To facilitate this, business applications and tools need to be interfaced with IT Service Management support tools to give the required functionality.

9.3 SERVICE AUTOMATION

Automation is to be considered to improve the utility and warranty of services.

9.3.1 Reasons for automation

Automation may offer advantages in many areas of opportunity, including the following:

- The capacity of automated resources can be more easily adjusted in response to variations in demand volumes.
- Automated resources can handle capacity with fewer restrictions on time of access.

- Automated systems present a good basis for measuring and improving service processes by holding constant the factor of human resources.
- Many optimization problems such as scheduling, routeing, and allocation of resources require computing power that is beyond the capacity of human agents.
- Automation is a means for capturing the knowledge required for a service process.

9.3.1.1 Preparing for automation

When automating, consider the following:

- Simplify the service processes before automating them.
- Clarify the flow of activities, allocation of tasks, need for information, and interactions.
- In self-service situations, reduce the surface area of the contact users have with the underlying systems and processes.
- Do not be in a hurry to automate tasks and interactions that are neither simple nor routine.

9.4   SERVICE ANALYTICS

Information is static. It only becomes knowledge when placed in the context of patterns and their implications. Those patterns give a high level of predictability and reliability on how the data will change over time. By understanding patterns of information we can answer 'How?' questions such as:

- How does this Incident affect the service?
- How is the business impacted?
- How do we respond?

This is Service Analytics.

Service Analytics is useful to model existing infrastructure components and support services to the higher-level business services. Infrastructure Events are then tied to corresponding business processes. The component-to-system-to-process linkage – also known as the Service Model – allows us to clearly identify the business impact of an Event.

Instead of responding to discrete Events, managers can characterize the behaviour of a service. This behaviour is then compared with a baseline of the normal behaviour for that time of day or business cycle.

With Service Analytics, not only can an operations group do a better job of identifying and correcting problems from the user's standpoint, but it can also predict the impact of changes to the environment. This same model can be turned around to show business demand for IT services. This is a high leverage point when building a dynamic provisioning or on-demand environment.

9.5   SAMPLE QUESTIONS AND ANSWERS

9.5.1   Questions

1   Which of the following requirements are adequate for an integrated set of Service Management technology?

　　1   The tool should have an integrated Configuration Management System to allow the organization's IT infrastructure assets, components and services to be held together with all relevant attributes and to allow relationships between each to be stored and maintained

　　2   The tool should be able to plan changes and assess the impact of changes to minimize the likelihood of post-production problems.

　　3   The tool should contain a workflow or process control engine to allow the pre-definition and control of defined processes such as an Incident Lifecycle, Request Fulfilment Lifecycle, Problem Lifecycle, Change model etc.

    4 The tool should ensure that all of the information within the Service Catalogue is accurate and up to date.

a 1 only

b 1 and 3 only

c 1, 3 and 4 only

d All of the above.

2 Which of the following should be considered when automating Service Management?

    1 Simplify the service processes before automating them.

    2 Clarify the flow of activities, allocation of tasks, need for information, and interactions.

    3 In self-service situations, reduce the surface area of the contact users have with the underlying systems and processes.

    4 Do not be in a hurry to automate tasks and interactions that are neither simple nor routine.

a 1 only

b 1 and 2 only

c 1, 2 and 3 only

d All of the above.

9.5.2 Answers

1 b – Option (2) and (4) are requirements for the processes and roles, and not the tool.

2 d – All these guidelines should be considered when applying automation.

How it all fits
together

10

10 How it all fits together

Each lifecycle stage is dependent on input from and provides output to the other stages in the lifecycle. The primary connection point between each of the lifecycle stages is the Service Portfolio. It is the 'spine' which connects the stages to each other.

10.1 KEY LINKS, INPUTS AND OUTPUTS

The Service Portfolio acts as the connection point or the spine of the Service Lifecycle (Figure 10.1). It is the single integrated source of information on the status of each service, other service details, and the interfaces and dependencies between services. The information within the Service Portfolio is used by the activities within each stage of the Service Lifecycle.

Figure 10.1 The Service Portfolio spine: key links, inputs and outputs in the Service Lifecycle

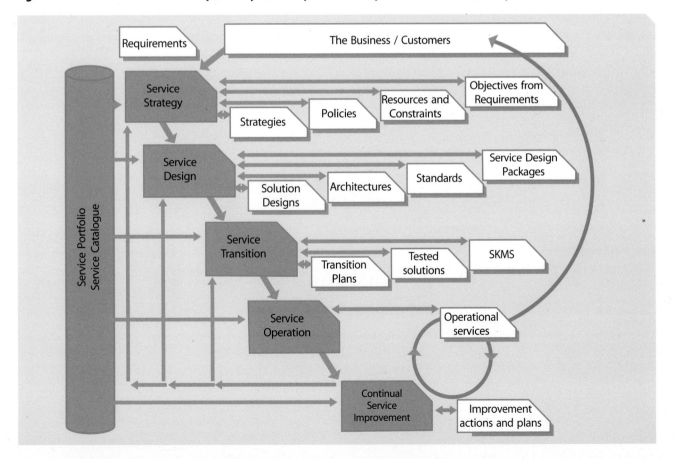

Figure 10.1 gives a good overview of the links, inputs and outputs involved at each stage of the Service Lifecycle. It illustrates the key outputs produced by each stage, which are used as inputs by the subsequent stages.

10.2 STRATEGY IMPLEMENTATION

For any given market space, Service Strategy defines the portfolio of services to be offered and the customers to be supported. This in turn determines the Service Portfolio that needs to be supported with design, transition and operation capabilities (Figure 10.2).

Lifecycle capabilities are defined in terms of the systems, processes, knowledge, skills and experience required at each phase to effectively support the Service Portfolios.

Interactions between Service Management Capabilities are clearly defined and managed for an integrated and systematic approach to Service Management.

Service Design and operation capabilities determine the type of transition capabilities required. They determine the portfolio of Service Designs and the operating range of the Service Provider in terms of models and capacities. Strategies are ultimately realized through Service Operation.

Transition capabilities determine the costs and risks managed by a Service Provider. How quickly a service is transitioned from design to operations depends on the capabilities of the Service Transition phase. Service Transition provides the decision analysis necessary to

Figure 10.2 Strategy implementation through the Service Lifecycle

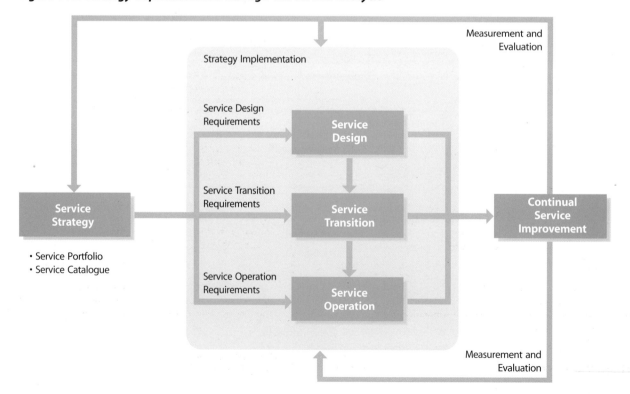

analyse, evaluate and approve strategic initiatives. In this manner, transition capabilities not only act as filters but also as amplifiers that increase the effectiveness of design and operation.

Service Strategy requires CSI to drive feedback through the Lifecycle elements to ensure that challenges and opportunities are not mismanaged.

10.3 SPECIALIZATION AND COORDINATION

Specialization and coordination are necessary in the lifecycle approach. Feedback and control between the functions and processes within and across the elements of the lifecycle make these possible. The dominant

pattern in the lifecycle is the sequential progress starting from Service Strategy through Service Delivery, Service Transition, Service Operation and CSI.

That, however, is not the only pattern of action. Every element of the lifecycle provides points for feedback and control (Figure 10.3).

10.4 MONITORING AND CONTROL

Each activity in a Service Management process should be monitored. The role of operational monitoring and control is to ensure that the process or service functions exactly as specified, which is why they are primarily concerned with maintaining the status quo.

Figure 10.3 Service Management processes are applied across the Service Lifecycle

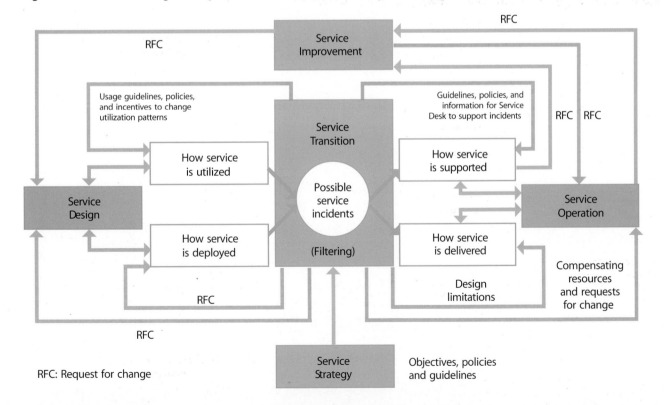

Figure 10.4 illustrates the monitoring and control of a process or of the components used to deliver a service.

The norms and monitoring and control mechanisms are defined in Service Design, but they are based on the standards and architectures defined during Service Strategy.

Notice that the second level of monitoring in this monitor control loop is performed by the CSI processes through Service Strategy and Service Design. These relationships are represented by the numbered arrows on the figure as follows:

Figure 10.4 Monitoring and control across the Service Lifecycle

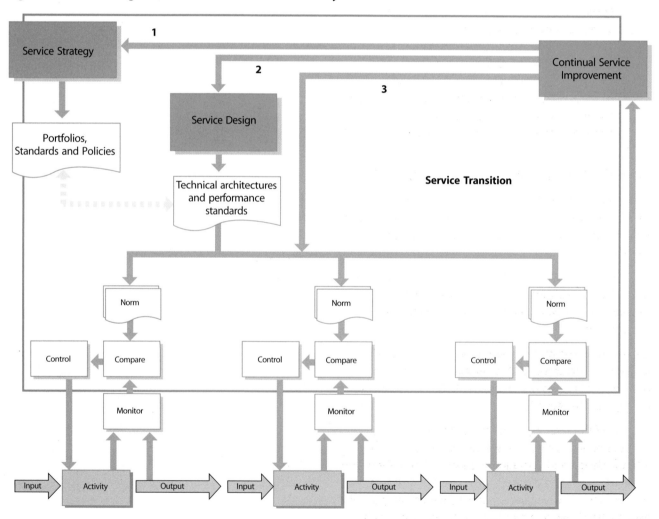

1 In this case CSI has recognized that the service will be improved by making a change to the Service Strategy. This could be the result of the business needing a change to the Service Portfolio, or that the architecture does not deliver what was expected.

2 In this case the SLRs need to be adjusted. It could be that the service is too expensive or because Operations Management is unable to maintain service quality in the current architecture.

3 In this case the norms specified in Service Design are not being adhered to. This could be because they are not appropriate or executable, or because of a lack of education or communication. The norms and the lack of compliance need to be investigated and action taken to rectify the situation.

10.5 CONTINUAL SERVICE IMPROVEMENT

An organization can find improvement opportunities throughout the entire Service Lifecycle. Figure 10.5 shows the interaction that should take place between each lifecycle phase.

An IT organization does not need to wait until a service or Service Management process is transitioned into the operations area to begin identifying improvement opportunities.

CSI will make use of the methods and practices found in many ITIL processes such as Problem Management, Availability Management and Capacity Management used throughout the lifecycle.

The use of the outputs, in the form of flows, matrices, statistics or analysis reports, will provide valuable insight into the design and operation of services. This information, combined with new business requirements, technology specifications, IT capabilities, budgets, trends and possibly external legislative and regulatory requirements, will be vital to CSI to determine what needs to be improved.

Figure 10.5 Continual Service Improvement throughout the Service Lifecycle

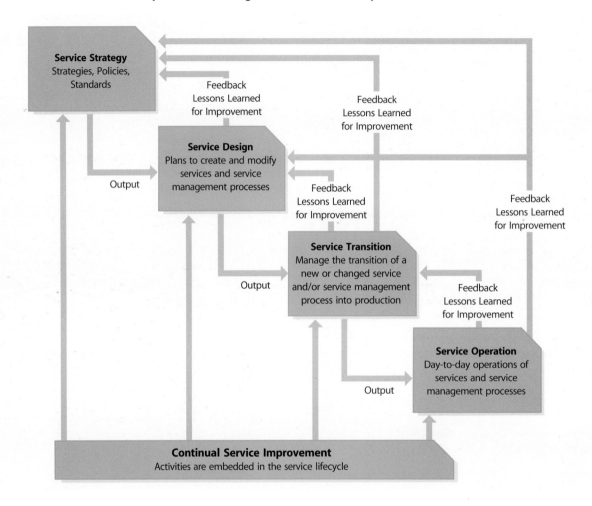

The examination and
exam preparation

11

11 The examination and exam preparation

11.1 THE EXAMINATION

The examination is a closed-book paper consisting of 40 multiple-choice questions. All 40 questions should be attempted. Each question has four choices, and the candidate must select one of these to answer a question.

The examination can be taken either on paper or online.

There is a maximum of 60 minutes to answer the paper. Candidates sitting the examination in a language other than their native language used in their business setting have a maximum of 75 minutes and are allowed to use a dictionary.

Candidates must answer 26 or more questions correctly to pass the examination, corresponding to a pass score of 65%.

If a candidate fails, they may retake the examination. There is no limit to the number of times a candidate may re-sit the examination.

11.2 EXAM PREPARATION

Attending an accredited Foundation training course is strongly recommended but not a prerequisite to sitting the examination. Candidates should note that the overall public examination pass rates are notably lower than the rates for candidates who have attended an accredited training course.

You should start preparing for the examination from the first day of the course. Use an effective note-taking system, and review the course material regularly. Transfer information to be learned onto note cards and review them every day.

Homework and self-study will be expected. Make appointments with yourself for study time.

Practise taking the examination to help familiarize yourself with it. You can use the sample tests in this publication, and your training provider will also provide you with recent sample papers. Because the examination is a timed test, you should prepare for your upcoming test under similar conditions. Make sure that whenever you take practice tests, you time yourself using the same amount of allotted time that will be allowed on the real test. Know in advance how many minutes you can spend per question and every few questions check yourself against the clock to see how you are doing.

Prepare far enough in advance so that you can actually relax the night before the exam.

During the examination:

- read each question carefully to make sure you understand the type of answer required
- come up with the answer in your head before looking at the possible answers
- read and consider all of the answer choices before you choose the one that best responds to the question
- make sure you answer the question that is being asked
- there will be no trick questions so do not waste time and energy looking for catch questions
- answer the easy questions first, then go back and answer the more difficult ones
- when attempting difficult questions, eliminate as many incorrect answers as you can, then make an educated guess from among those remaining
- do not spend too much time on any one question
- check that you have answered every question. Your scores on the multiple-choice tests are based on the number of questions you answer correctly. There is no penalty for guessing

- review your work. If you finish a test before time is up, go back and check your work
- do not keep on changing an answer – usually your first choice is the right one, unless you misread the question.

Sample ITIL version 3 Foundation examination

12 Sample ITIL version 3 Foundation examination

12.1 SAMPLE QUESTIONS

12.1.1 Instructions

All 40 questions should be attempted.

There are no trick questions.

You have 60 minutes to complete this paper. Candidates sitting the examination in a language other than their native language have a maximum of 75 minutes and are allowed the use of a dictionary.

You must get 26 or more answers correct to pass.

More sample papers can be requested from your course provider.

12.1.2 Questions

1 Which of the following statements BEST describes one of the purposes of Service Analytics?
   a Service Analytics is a means for automating simple and routine tasks and interactions.
   b Service Analytics is useful to restore normal Service Operation as quickly as possible in case of an Incident.
   c Service Analytics is useful to model existing components and services to the higher-level business services.
   d Service Analytics is a means to ensure proper funding for the delivery and consumption of services.

2 The goal of Problem Management is:
   a to prevent Problems and resulting Incidents from happening
   b to provide a channel for users to request standard services
   c to restore normal Service Operation as quickly as possible
   d to detect Events, make sense of them, and determine the appropriate control action.

3 Which of the following statements BEST describes the role of the Service Desk as the single point of contact?
   a All requests, such as Incidents, Service Requests and Service Level Requirements from users and customers must pass through the Service Desk
   b To provide a single point of contact to the users, an organization can only have one centralized Service Desk.
   c As a user I have one single point of contact for all my Incidents and Service Requests but other users in the organization may have other points of contact.
   d The Service Desk is on offer for the users in an organization. But they are of course allowed to contact anybody within the IT organization with their Incidents and Service Requests.

4 Which of the following statements about the Process Owner role are CORRECT?
   1 Every person involved in a process is a Process Owner.
   2 The Process Owner is responsible for ensuring that the process is meeting the aims of the process definition.

3 The Process Owner and Process Manager roles are always undertaken by the same person.

4 Process Ownership is always a role as well as a function in any organization.

a 2 only

b 2 and 3 only

c 2, 3 and 4 only

d All of the above.

5 Which of the following is NOT an activity in the Change Management process?

b Review the Request for Change

c Plan updates

d Change Design

e Assess and evaluate change.

6 Which of the following are goals and objectives for the Service Level Management process?

1 To provide and improve the relationship and communication with the business and customers.

2 To produce and maintain an appropriate and up-to-date Capacity Plan which reflects the current and future needs of the business.

3 To ensure that proactive measures to improve the levels of service delivered are implemented.

4 To support efficient and effective business and Service Management processes by providing accurate information about assets.

a a 1 only

b b 1 and 3 only

c c 1, 2 and 3 only

d d All of the above.

7 Which of the following metrics types is NOT a typical type of metrics?

a Technology metrics

b Service Metrics

c Baseline metrics

d Process metrics.

8 Which of the following validation activities BEST corresponds to the definition of customer and business requirements (level 1) in the Service V-model?

a Validate Service Packages, offerings and contracts

b Service operational readiness test

c Service Release Package test

d Component and assembly test.

9 Which of the following statements BEST describes the difference between an Operational Level Agreement and an Underpinning Contract?

a Only the Operational Level Agreement is an underpinning agreement between an IT Service Provider and another part of the same organization that assists with the provision of services.

b Only the Operational Level Agreement defines the goods or services to be provided and the responsibilities of both parties.

c Only the Underpinning Contract defines targets and responsibilities that are required to meet agreed Service Level Targets in a Service Level Agreement.

d Only the Underpinning Contract supports the IT Service Provider's delivery of IT services to customers

10 Which of the following goals are the primary goals for Service Operation?

1 To allow for changes and improvement.

2 To design processes for the operation of IT services.

3 To achieve effectiveness and efficiency in the delivery and support of services.

4 To maintain stability.

a 3 only

b 3 and 4 only

c 1, 3 and 4 only

d All of the above.

11 Which of the following is the CORRECT definition of Service Management?
   a Service Management is a set of specialized organizational resources for providing value to customers in the form of services.
   b Service Management is a set of specialized organizational resources for providing value to customers in the form of goods and products.
   c Service Management is a set of specialized organizational capabilities for providing value to customers in the form of services.
   d Service Management is a set of specialized organizational capabilities for providing value to the Service Provider in the form of goods and products.

12 Consider the following types of technological support of Service Management and the corresponding descriptions.
   A Technology-assisted
   B Technology-facilitated
   C Technology-mediated
   D Technology-generated (self-service)
   1 The Service Provider is represented entirely by technology.
   2 The Service Provider and the customer are not in physical proximity.
   3 Only the Service Provider has access to the technology.
   4 Both the Service Provider and the customer have access to the same technology.

   Which of the following pairings between roles and responsibilities is CORRECT?
   a A–3, B–1, C–2 and D–4
   b A–1, B–2, C–3 and D–4
   c A–3, B–4, C–2 and D–1
   d A–4, B–3, C–2 and D–1

13 Which of the following is NOT described as a function but as a process in the ITIL Service Management Practices framework?
   a Technical Management
   b Service Portfolio Management
   c Service Desk
   d Applications Management.

14 Which of the following roles may be involved in the Continual Service Improvement process?
   1 The Continual Service Improvement Manager
   2 The customer
   3 The Service Manager
   4 The Process Owners
   a 1 only
   b 1 and 3 only
   c 1, 3 and 4 only
   d All of the above.

15 Which of the following statements BEST describes prioritization in the Incident Management process?
   a Prioritization is determined by the urgency of the Incident and the level of impact the Incident is causing.
   b Prioritization is determined by the resources available and the level of impact the Incident is causing.
   c Prioritization is determined by the resources available and the urgency of the Incident.
   d Prioritization is determined by the resources available, the urgency of the Incident and the level of impact the Incident is causing.

16 Which of the following questions is NOT one of the 7 Rs that must be answered for all changes as part of the impact assessment?
   a What RESOURCES are required to deliver the change?
   b Who RAISED the change?
   c What is the RELATIONSHIP between this change and other changes?

d Who is going to REVIEW the change when it has been implemented?

17 The BEST way to define the services in the Service Portfolio is to base the definitions on:
a the resources needed to deliver the service
b the business outcome of the service
c the capabilities needed to deliver the service
d the composition of the service.

18 Which of the following statements is the CORRECT description of the 'Act' stage in the Deming Cycle for quality improvement?
a At this stage goals and measures are established.
b At this stage the implemented improvements are compared to the measures of success.
c At this stage it is determined to keep the status quo, close the gap or add necessary resources.
d At this stage a project to close identified gaps is developed and implemented.

19 Which of the following questions helps identifying what a customer values?
1 Who is our customer?
2 Who depends on our services?
3 How does the customer use our services?
4 What do we provide?
a 1 only
b 1 and 3 only
c 1, 2 and 3 only
d All of the above.

20 The goal of Continual Service Improvement is BEST described as:
a to continually align and re-align IT services to the changing business needs by identifying and implementing improvements to IT services that support business processes
b to encourage Service Providers to stop and think why something is to be done before thinking how

c to continually identify and implement improvements to IT components that support the general technological developments.
d to design services that satisfy business objectives.

21 Which of the following are generic elements of a process?
1 Process activities
2 Process policy
3 Process roles
4 Process metrics.
a 1 only
b 1 and 3 only
c 1, 3 and 4 only
d All of the above.

22 Which of the following statements are CORRECT regarding the RACI authority matrix?
1 The 'R' in RACI stands for 'Responsible'.
2 The RACI chart shows the activities down the left-hand side and the functional roles across the top.
3 More than one person can be accountable for each task.
4 The 'I' in RACI stands for 'Initiator'.
a 1 only
b 1 and 2 only
c 1, 2 and 3 only
d All of the above.

23 Which of the following is NOT an activity that IT Operations Management is responsible for?
a Console management
b Management of facilities
c Output management
d Maintenance of a stable technical infrastructure.

24 Assume that IT Operations is separated from Technical and Application Management. Which of the following roles does Technical and Application Management normally NOT play in the Event Management process?

a Participating in the instrumentation of the services.

b Testing the services to ensure that Events are properly generated.

c Ensuring that any auto responses are defined.

d Monitoring Events.

25 Which of the following statements are CORRECT about Service Asset and Configuration Management?

    1 Configuration Management delivers a logical model of the services, assets and the infrastructure.

    2 Information about each Configuration Item is recorded in a configuration record in the Configuration Management System.

    3 The Service Knowledge Management System includes the Configuration Management System and databases, as well as other tools and databases.

    4 Status Accounting and Reporting is an activity in the Service Asset and Configuration Management process.

a 1 only

b 1 and 2 only

c 1, 2 and 3 only.

d All of the above

26 Which of the following statements BEST describes the goals of Supplier Management?

    1 To ensure that underpinning contracts and agreements with suppliers are aligned to business needs and managed through their lifecycle.

    2 To manage relationships with suppliers.

    3 To ensure that that the information security risks are appropriately managed and enterprise information resources are used responsibly.

    4 To maintain a supplier policy and a supporting Supplier and Contract Database.

a 1 only

b 1 and 2 only

c 1, 2 and 4 only

d All of the above.

27 Which of the following activities BEST help an organization managing and developing Service Management as a strategic asset?

    1 Identification of critical services across the Service Portfolio for a given customer or market space.

    2 Establishment of the right mix of services to offer to customers.

    3 Tagging all service assets with the name of the services to which they add service potential.

    4 Creation of diagnostic scripts for diagnosis of Incidents.

a 1 only

b 1 and 2 only

c 1, 2 and 3 only

d All of the above.

28 A key role for Service Operation is to achieve a balance between conflicting sets of priorities. A fundamental conflict exists between IT as a set of technology components on one side and:

a the view in which the organization focuses only on business requirements and the services delivered

b the ability to respond to change without impacting on other services

c a strong focus on delivering quality

d proactive behaviour on the other side.

29 When should a Service Design Package be produced?

a During the strategy stage, for each time a new service is added to the Service Portfolio.

b During the design stage, for each change to a service or removal of a service.

c When a new or changed service is passed from Service Design to Service Transition.

d During the design stage, for each new service, major change to a service or removal of a service.

30 Which of the following benefits is NOT primarily the result of good Service Design practices?

  a Reduced total cost of ownership.

  b More effective Service Management processes.

  c Increased success rate of changes and releases for the business.

  d Improved quality and consistency of service.

31 ITIL is BEST characterized as:

  a An international standard

  b Good practice

  c A qualification scheme

  d Academic research.

32 Which of the following activities is the Service Owner of a specific service responsible for?

  1 Representing the service in Change Advisory Board meetings.

  2 Participating in negotiating Service Level Agreements.

  3 Defining the process strategy.

  4 Liaising with the appropriate Process Owners.

  a 1 only

  b 1 and 2 only

  c 1, 2 and 4 only

  d All of the above.

33 Which of the following is the CORRECT order of the activities in the 7-Step Improvement Process (first activity first)?

  a 1 – Define what you should measure. 2 – Define what you can measure. 3 – Gather data. 4 – Process data. 5 – Analyse data. 6 – Present information. 7 – Implement corrective action.

  b 1 – Define what you can measure. 2 – Define what you should measure. 3 – Gather data. 4 – Analyse data. 5 – Process data. 6 – Present information. 7 – Implement corrective action.

  c 1 – Define what you should measure. 2 – Define what you can measure. 3 – Gather data. 4 – Analyse data. 5 – Process data. 6 – Present information. 7 – Implement corrective action.

  d 1 – Define what you can measure. 2 – Define what you should measure. 3 – Gather data. 4 – Process data. 5 – Analyse data. 6 – Present information. 7 – Implement corrective action.

34 Which of the following methods is NOT a deployment approach?

  a Big-bang

  b Phased

  c Pull

  d Request.

35 Which of the following activities forms part of the Service Portfolio Management process?

  1 Analyse

  2 Define

  3 Approve

  4 Charter.

  a 1 only

  b 1 and 2 only

  c 1, 2 and 3 only

  d All of the above.

36 To answer the question 'Where do we want to be?' in the Continual Service Improvement model, we need to know:

  1 The vision of the organization

  2 The mission of the business

  3 The current baseline

  4 The metrics.

  a 1 only

  b 1 and 2 only

  c 1, 2 and 3 only

  d All of the above.

37 Good Service Design is dependent on effective and efficient use of the four Ps – people, processes, partners and:
   a   plans
   b   products
   c   practices
   d   policies.

38 Which is the best description of a Service Catalogue?
   a   A document defining all aspects of an IT Service and its requirements through each stage of its lifecycle.
   b   The complete set of services that are managed by a Service Provider.
   c   A database or structured document with information about all live IT services, including those available for deployment.
   d   An agreement between an IT Service Provider and the IT customer(s).

39 Which of the following statements are CORRECT about utility and warranty?
   1   Utility can be described as what the customer gets.
   2   Warranty can be defined as 'fitness for use'.
   3   Utility increases the average performance.
   4   Warranty reduces the variation in performance.
   a   1 only
   b   1 and 2 only
   c   1, 2 and 3 only
   d   All of the above.

40 The Service Portfolio is the single integrated source of information on the status, interfaces and dependencies of each service used by activities within the following stages in the Service Lifecycle:
   1   Service Strategy
   2   Service Transition
   3   Service Design
   4   Service Operation.

   a   1 only
   b   1 and 2 only
   c   1, 2 and 3 only
   d   All of the above.

12.2 ANSWERS TO SAMPLE QUESTIONS

1   c – Option (a) is an objective for Event Management, (b) is an objective for Incident Management and (d) is an objective for Financial Management.

2   a – Option (b) is a goal for Request Fulfilment, (c) is a goal for Incident Management and (d) is a goal for Event Management.

3   c – Single point of contact is seen from the user's perspective. Option (a) is incorrect because customer requests such as Service Level Requirements normally go to a Business Relationship Manager, a Service Level Manager or similar. Option (b) is incorrect because different users can contact different Service Desks as long as each user has only one single contact point. Option (d) is incorrect because single point of contact is also a means to ensure that all user requests are logged and tracked by a dedicated function.

4   a – Only the person responsible for the process as a whole is the Process Owner; the Process Owner and Process Manager (i.e. Incident Manager) can be the same person, but is not necessarily the same person; and Process Ownership is always a role but is not necessarily implemented as a function in the organization.

5   c – There is no activity in the Change Management process for managing individual changes called 'Change Design'.

6   b – Option 2 is an objective for Capacity Management and option 4 is an objective for Service Asset and Configuration Management.

7 c – Baselines are markers or starting points for later comparisons of measurements.

8 a – Option (b) corresponds to level 3 (define Service Solution), option (c) corresponds to level 4 (define Service Release) and option (d) corresponds to level 5 (develop Service Solution).

9 a – Option (b), (c) and (d) are true for both types of agreement.

10 c – Option 2, design of processes, is a goal for Service Design.

11 c – Service Management is a set of specialized organizational capabilities for providing value to customers in the form of services.

12 c

13 b – Service Portfolio Management is described as a process, whereas Technical Management, Service Desk and Applications Management are described as functions in the Service Operation volume.

14 d – Not only all the internal roles in the Service Provider organization but also the customers should be involved in Continual Service Improvement.

15 a – The resources available are not determining the prioritization of the Incident. Constraints to resources are the reason to do the prioritization.

16 d – The review and close of the change is not part of the impact assessment.

17 b – An outcome-based definition of services ensures that the organization plans and executes all aspects of Service Management entirely from the perspective of what is valuable to the customer.

18 c – Option (a) is a description of the 'Plan 'stage, option (b) is a description of the 'Check' stage and option (d) is a description of the 'Do' stage.

19 c – Knowledge of the Service Provider's current services does not help identifying what a customer values.

20 a – Option (b) is the goal for Service Strategy, option (c) focuses on technological developments instead of the business needs and the supporting IT services, and option (d) is an objective for Service Design.

21 d – All of the stated elements forms part of a process as well as procedures, work instructions, triggers, input, output, capabilities etc.

22 b – More than one person can be responsible for each task but only one person can be accountable for each task. 'I' stands for 'Informed'.

23 d – Technical Management, not IT Operations Management, is responsible for planning, implementing and maintaining a stable technical infrastructure.

24 d – Where IT Operations is separated from Technical and Application Management, IT Operations is commonly delegated the Event monitoring and first-line response activities.

25 d – All of the statements are true about Service Asset and Configuration Management.

26 c – Even though it is important to manage information security risks for data and services managed by third parties (option 3), this is a responsibility for the Information Security Management process.

27 c – Options 1, 2 and 3 are all part of the activities involved in developing Service Management as a strategic asset within the Service Strategy Management process. Option 4 improves the Service Management processes but not necessarily as a strategic asset.

28 a – The other options are counterparts of stability, cost and reactive behaviour, respectively.

29 d – The Service Design Package should be produced during the design stage for new, changed and removed services. A Service Design package is normally only produced for major changes.

30 c – An increased rate of success of changes and releases is first and foremost a result of good Service Transition practices. The (a) total cost of ownership is reduced as a result of well-designed services, processes and technology, (b) more effective processes are a result of processes designed with optimal quality and cost effectiveness and (d) improved quality and consistency of service are the result of services designed within the corporate strategy, architecture and constraints.

31 b – ITIL is an example of good practice. (a) ISO/IEC 20000 provides a formal standard for organizations seeking to have their Service Management Capabilities audited and certified, (c) the IT Service Management certifications and diplomas owned by OGC and managed by APMG form an example of a qualification scheme and (d) there are good examples of academic research supporting and/or criticizing ITIL but ITIL itself is not academic research.

32 c – Defining the process strategy is a responsibility of the Process Owner, whereas the Service Owner is responsible for the three other activities.

33 a

34 d – A deployment method called 'Request' does not exist in ITIL. Option (a) is where the new or changed service is deployed to all user areas in one operation, (b) is where the service is deployed to a part of the user base initially and the this operation is repeated for subsequent parts of the user base, and (c) is where the software is available in a central location but users are free to download the software at a time of their choosing.

35 d – All of the activities are part of the Service Portfolio Management process.

36 c – The answer to the question 'Where do we want to be?' involves measurable targets, which are the prerequisites for defining the metrics. We therefore only need to know the vision, mission, goals, objectives and baseline to answer the question.

37 b – Good Service Design is dependent on all four answers, but the last 'P' in the 'four Ps' tenet stands for 'products'.

38 c – The others are definitions of (a) a Service Design Package, (b) a Service Portfolio and (d) a Service Level Agreement.

39 d – All of the statements are true for utility and warranty.

40 d – The Service Portfolio acts as the connection point or the 'spine' of all five stages in the Service Lifecycle.

References and
useful websites

References and useful websites

REFERENCES

The official ITIL Service Management Practices framework

- *Official Introduction to the ITIL Service Lifecycle* (ISBN: 9780113310616)
- *Service Strategy* (ISBN: 9780113310456)
- *Service Design* (ISBN: 9780113310470)
- *Service Transition* (ISBN: 9780113310487)
- *Service Operation* (ISBN: 9780113310463)
- *Continual Service Improvement* (ISBN: 9780113310494)

ISO/IEC 20000 publications

- *A Manager's Guide to Service Management*. 2nd edition (updated for BS ISO/IEC 20000) (ISBN: 0580479226)
- *BS ISO/IEC 20000–1:2005 IT Service Management – Part 1: Specification* (ISBN: 0580475298)
- *BS ISO/IEC 20000–2:2005 IT Service Management – Part 2: Code of Practice* (ISBN: 0580475301)
- *IT Service Management A Self-assessment Workbook* (BIP 0015–2005) (ISBN: 0580479234)
- BS ISO/IEC 27001:2005(E) (BS 7799–2:2005) Information technology – Security techniques – Information security management systems – Requirements
- BS ISO/IEC 17799:2005 (BS 7799–1:2005) Information technology – Security techniques – Code of Practice for Information Security Management

USEFUL WEBSITES

ITIL

- http://www.itil.com
- http://www.itil-officialsite.com

Certification

- http://www.apmgroup.co.uk
- http://www.bcs.org/iseb
- http://www.exin-exams.com

ISO/IEC 20000

- http://www.isoiec20000certification.com

*it*SMF International

- http://www.itsmf.org

Index

Index

Page references for figures and tables are in *italics*.

7-Step Improvement Process 107–11, *107, 108, 109*

access 90
Access Management 90–1
accounting 36
Accredited Training Organizations (ATOs) 6
activity metrics 107
Alerts 83
APM Group (APMG) 5, 6
Application Management 84, 91, 96–7
Application Service Providers (ASPs) 47
applications 15
Applications Architecture 45
architecture 41, 42, 45, *46*
audit 70
automation 76, 117–18
availability 13, 54
Availability Management 54–5, *55, 56*
Availability Manager 55

baselines 106
benefits 103
big-bang 75
Business Architecture 45, *46*
Business Capacity Management 53
business case 30–1, *31*
Business Continuity Management 56, 57, *57*
Business Impact Analysis 57
business process 15
business process outsourcing 47
Business Service Catalogue 48, *48*
Business Service Management 117
business value
    Continual Service Improvement 103

Service Design 41–2
Service Operation 81
Service Transition 65

capabilities 13, *13*, 21
    service potential 33
    value creation 29
Capacity Management 53–4, *53*
Capacity Manager 54
CCTA (Central Computer and Telecommunications Agency) 5
Centralized Service Desk 92–3, *93*
Change Advisory Board (CAB) 20, 71, 73
Change Management 63, *64*, 71–3, *72*
Change Manager 73
Changes 71
    types 71, *72*
closed-loop systems 16, *17*
co-sourcing 47
communication 83
Complementary Guidance 25
compliance 36, 45
Component Capacity Management 53
Configuration Administrator/Librarian 70
Configuration Analyst 70
configuration control 70
configuration identification 70
Configuration Items (CIs) 48, 66
Configuration Management 33, 63, *64*, 65–70
Configuration Management Database (CMDB) *75*
Configuration Management System (CMS) 52, 69, *69*
    integrated 117
Configuration Management System/Tools Administrator 70
Configuration Manager 70
Continual Service Improvement (CSI) 4, 25, 26, 103
    business value 103
    goals and objectives 103

key principles 103–7
processes 107–11
sample questions and answers 111–12
scope 103
through Service Lifecycle 125, 127, *128*
Continual Service Improvement (CSI) Manager 111
Continual Service Improvement (CSI) model 105–6, *105*
Continuity Plans 57
control 125–7, *126*
Core Service Packages 36
core services 14
cost, and quality 82
cost classifications 36
cost types 36
critical success factors (CSFs) 107, 109

dashboards 117
data 15, 108
Data Architecture 45
Definitive Media Library 74–5, *75*
Demand Management 35–6
demand modelling 36
Deming cycle 104–5, *104*
CSI model 105–6, *105*
Deployment Manager 77
deployment technology 117
diagnostic utilities 117
discovery technology 117

effectiveness 46
efficiency 46
Emergency Change 71
Enterprise Architecture 45, *46*
environment 15
Environmental Architecture 45
Event Management 83–4
Events 83
Incident Management 84
examination 131

preparation 131–2
sample 135–43
Examination Institute for Information Science (EXIN) 6
Examination Institutes 5, 6
websites 147
exceptions 84
External Service Provider 49

Facilities Management 96
Financial Management 36
Follow-the-Sun 92, 93
functional escalation 86
functions 19

goals 109
governance 103–4

hierarchic escalation 86

identity 90
improvements 103
Incident lifecycle view 53, *54*
Incident Management 84–6, *86*, *87*, 88
Service Requests 89
Incident Manager 88
Incident Models 85
Incidents 53, 84
categorization 85
closure 88
diagnosis 86
escalation 86
identification 85
investigation and diagnosis 86
logging 85
prioritization 86
resolution and recovery 88
information 108–9
Information Architecture 45
Information Security Management 57–8, *58*

Information Security Management System (ISMS) 58
Information Security Policy 58
Information Systems Examination Board (ISEB) 6
informational events 83
infrastructure 15
insourcing 47
Internal Service Provider 49
ISO/IEC 20000 21
    publications 147
    website 147
IT Dansk (ITD) 6
IT governance 103–4
IT Infrastructure Architecture 45
IT Operations Management 96
    Access Management 91
    Event Management 83, 84
    and Technical Management 96
IT Service Management *see* Service Management
IT Service Management Forum 6, 147
ITIL 3, 21
    Qualification Scheme 3–8, *3*
    websites 147
ITIL Advanced Service Management Professional certificate 5
ITIL Complementary Guidance 25
ITIL Core 25
ITIL Foundation certificate 4, 6–7
    examination and exam preparation 131–2
    sample examination 135–43
ITIL Intermediate qualification certificates 4
ITIL Service Management Practices 25, 147
ITIL Service Management Professional (ISMP) certificate 4, 5
*it*SMF 6, 147

key performance indicators (KPIs) 20, 107, 109, 110–11
knowledge 109
Knowledge Management 63, *64*
knowledge process outsourcing 47
Known Error Database 90
Known Error Records 85

Known Errors 63, 89

licensing technology 117
lifecycle *see* Service Lifecycle
Local Service Desk 92, *92*
Loyalist Certification Services (LCS) 6

manual mechanism 76
market space 33
measurement 106–7, *106*
metrics 109
process activities 110
    metrics 107, 109
    mission statement 109
monitoring 125–7, *126*
multisourcing 47

Normal Change 71, *72*

objectives 34, 109
OGC (Office of Government Commerce) 5
Operational Level Agreements (OLAs) 15, 49, *49*, 50
Operational Monitoring and Control 83
Operational Support and Analysis 4
Operations Control 96
Operations Management *see* IT Operations Management
outsourcing 47

partnership 47
Patterns of Business Activity 35
performance average 13
performance potential 33
performance variation 14
phased approach 75
planning 36
Planning, Protection and Optimization 4
privileges 90–1
proactive organizations 83
Problem Management 89–90

Problem Manager 90
Problem Models 90
Problems 89
process control engine 116
process metrics 107
Process Owner 20
processes 15–16
    closed-loop systems 16, *17*
    process characteristics 18
    process model 17, *18*
progress 45
Pull approach 76
Push approach 76

qualifications bodies 5–6
    websites 147
qualitative key performance indicators 110
quality, and cost 82
quantitative key performance indicators 110–11

RACI 19–20, *19*
RACI-VS 20
reactive organizations 83
Release and Deployment Management 74–7, *74*, *75*, 76
Release and Deployment Manager 76–7
Release, Control and Validation 4
Release Packaging and Build Manager 77
Release Units 74, *74*
remote control 117
reporting 117
Request Fulfilment 88–9
Request Model 89
Requests for Change (RFCs) 20, 71, 73
resolution 90
resources 13, *13*
    Application Management 97
    service potential 33
    Technical Management 95
    value creation 29

responsiveness 82
retired services 44, *44*
rights 90–1
risk 31, *32*
risk analysis 31, *32*
risk management 31, *32*
roles 19
    RACI 19–20, *19*

security controls 58
Security Manager 58
security organization 58
Security Strategy 58
self-help capabilities 116
Service Analytics *107*, 108–9, *108*, 118
Service Architecture 45
Service Asset and Configuration Management 63, *64*, 65–70
Service Asset Manager 70
service assets 11, 13
service automation 117–18
Service Capability 4
Service Capacity Management 53
Service Catalogue 30, *30*, 33, 36
    management 47–8, *48*
    Service Design 41, 44, *44*
    suppliers 52
Service Catalogue Manager 48
Service Continuity Management 56–7, *57*
Service Continuity Manager 57
Service Design 4, 25, 26, 41, 124
    business value 41–2
    Event Management 84
    goals and objectives 41
    key principles 42–7
    processes 47–58
    sample questions and answers 59–60
    scope 41
    Technical and Application Management teams 91

tools 116
Service Design Package 42
Service Desk 7
    Access Management 91
    Incident Management 85, 86, 88
    metrics 95
    objectives 91–2
    organizational structures 92–3, *92*, *93*, *94*
    Request Fulfilment 89
    role 91
    staffing 94–5
Service Investment Analysis 36
Service Knowledge Management System (SKMS) 52, 67, *68*, 69
Service Level Agreements (SLAs) 15, 49, *49*, 51
Service Level Management 48–52, *50*
Service Level Manager 51–6
Service Level Packages 36
Service Level Requirements (SLRs) 15
Service Lifecycle 4, 7, 25–6, *25*, 123
    Continual Service Improvement 127, *128*
    key links, inputs and outputs 123–4
    monitoring and control 125–7
    sample question and answer 26
    specialization and coordination 125
    strategy implementation 124–5
    support and assistance 116
Service Management 11, 12–13, *12*
    good practice 21
    ITIL Qualification Scheme 3–8
    processes, functions and roles 15–21, 81
    resources and capabilities 13
    sample questions and answers 21–2
    Service Packages 14–15
    utility and warranty 13–14
Service Management Technology 115–16, *115*
    automation 117–18
    generic requirements 116–17
    sample questions and answers 118–19

Service Analytics 118
Service Manager 111
service metrics 107
Service Model 118
Service Offerings and Agreements 4
Service Operation 4, 25, 26, 81
    business value 81
    functions 91–7
    goals and objectives 81
    key principles 81–3
    processes 83–91
    sample questions and answers 97–9
    scope 81
Service Owner 20–1
Service Packages 14–15, *15*, 16, *16*
Service Pipeline 33, 44, *44*
Service Portfolio 30, *30*, 33, 123, *123*
    Service Design 41, 42, 44, *44*
    and Service Strategy 124
    suppliers 52
Service Portfolio Management 35, *35*
service potential 33
Service Providers 49
Service Provisioning Optimization (SPO) 36
service recording 36
Service Requests 89
    see also Request Fulfilment
Service Strategy 4, 25, 26, 29
    goals and objectives 29
    key principles 30–1, *30*, *32*
    processes 32–6
    sample questions and answers 37
    scope 29
    Supplier Management 52
    through Service Lifecycle 124–5
    value creation 29
Service Transition 4, 25, 26, 63, 124–5
    business value 65
    Event Management 84

goals and objectives 63
key principles 65, *66*
processes 65–77
sample questions and answers 77–8
scope 63, *64*
Technical and Application Management teams 91
services 11, *11*, *12*, 15
Service Design 41
Shared Services Unit 49
skills 94–5
sourcing strategies 47
stability 82
Standard Change 71, 89
status accounting and reporting 70
strategies 34
strategy generation 32–4, *34*
super users 95
Supplier and Contracts Database 52
Supplier Management 52–3, *52*
Supplier Manager 52–3
suppliers 15, 50–1
support services 15
support teams 15
supporting services 14

Technical Management 84, 91, 95–6, 97
Technical Service Catalogue 48, *48*
technology 81
  see also Service Management Technology
technology metrics 107
Tools Administrator 70
training 95

Underpinning Contracts 49, *49*, 50
utility 13, *14*

value creation 29
verification, Service Asset and Configuration Management 70
Virtual Service Desk 92, 93, *94*
vision 109

warning events 83–4
warranty 13–14, *14*
wisdom 109
Workarounds 84, 85
  Known Errors 89
workflow 116

Best Management Practice™

For Project, Programme,
Risk and Service Management

20% discount on core ITIL publications

To help you continue to learn and develop your ITIL knowledge and IT service management skills we are offering you a 20% discount on the ITIL Lifecycle Publication Suite and the Official Introduction to The ITIL Service Lifecycle. This offer is available on both the Hardcopy and the Online Subscription. For further information on these products visit:
www.best-management-practice.com

To benefit from this offer simply call our customer services team on **0870 6005522** and quote **STU** or visit **www.best-management-practice. com/Online-Bookshop/IT-Service-Management-ITIL/** and enter **STU1** in the promotional code box on the Shopping Basket page.

20% DISCOUNT